HOME-MADE·
for HOLIDAYS
the

Over 60 Treats to Enjoy at Home or Give as Gifts

Aileen A. Anastacio

Angelo F. Comsti

 **Marshall Cavendish**
Cuisine

Editor: Lydia Leong
Designer: Adithi Khandadi
Photographer: At Maculangan, Pioneer Studios

Text © 2012 Marshall Cavendish International (Asia) Private Limited,
Aileen A. Anastacio and Angelo F. Comsti
Photographs © 2012 Marshall Cavendish International (Asia) Private Limited

Published by Marshall Cavendish Cuisine
An imprint of Marshall Cavendish International

Other Marshall Cavendish Offices:
Marshall Cavendish International. PO Box 65829, London, EC1P 1NY, UK • Marshall
Cavendish Corporation, 99 White Plains Road, Tarrytown NY 10591-9001, USA •
Marshall Cavendish International (Thailand) Co Ltd. 253 Asoke, 12th Flr, Sukhumvit
21 Road, Klongtoey Nua, Wattana, Bangkok 10110, Thailand • Marshall Cavendish
(Malaysia) Sdn Bhd, Times Subang, Lot 46, Subang Hi-Tech Industrial Park, Batu Tiga,
40000 Shah Alam, Selangor Darul Ehsan, Malaysia

Marshall Cavendish is a trademark of Times Publishing Limited

National Library Board, Singapore Cataloguing-in-Publication Data

Anastacio, Aileen A.
Home-made for the holidays : over 60 treats to enjoy at home or give as gifts / Aileen A.
Anastacio, Angelo F. Comsti. – Singapore : Marshall Cavendish Cuisine, c2012.
p. cm.
ISBN : 978-981-4361-22-4

1. Holiday cooking. I. Comsti, Angelo F. II. Title.

TX739
641.568 -- dc22   OCN750842831

Printed in Singapore by KWF Printing Pte Ltd

This book is for you my sweetie, Sabrina.
My holidays have been merrier since I had you.
You have always been my source of inspiration,
my number one fan and most of all, my official
food taster. I look forward to celebrating more
holidays with you.

This book is also dedicated to my nephew Nico
and my nieces Danie, Sophie and baby Zoe.

Aileen

This book is for my parents who wholeheartedly back me up in all my endeavours. Your love and support drive me to do far greater things because I know you'll be there beside me. I hope I've made you proud.

Also, to my honest critics and solid support system—Carlo, Paolo, Ria, Angela and my nephews Pocholo and Joaquin. Thank you for adding fuel to the flame.

Angelo

Contents

Acknowledgements

This book is the result of a healthy collaboration of a team whose individual talents and passions have both impressed and inspired us. Our thanks go to:

At Maculangan, who brings the best out of food when it comes to photography. Your attention to detail and desire to produce a commendable quality of work are truly noteworthy and much appreciated.

Jacqueline Franquelli, who never fails to put into words what we sometimes can't. We are truly grateful as you always find a way to fix and fine-tune our loose ends.

Our families and friends, for bearing with us on our late nights and for pushing us to go the extra mile. Your prayers, support, comments and suggestions never go unnoticed.

And of course, our Almighty God, for always guiding us, especially when we need it most.

Introduction

This book wasn't really something we set out to do right from the get-go. What started out as an idea mentioned in passing over crêpes and coffee snowballed into the realisation of this cookbook. With just two weeks to work on everything, this project seemed like an impossible feat or for people who get turned on with challenges, a most welcome dare. Unfortunately, we are among those crazy fools.

We soon found ourselves madly scouring the city for holiday-themed props, baking fruit cake and gingerbread cookies in the middle of a hot and humid July, and pulling five straight all-nighters to keep to our tight production schedule. Yet, in the middle of the mad rush, we somehow managed to take in and share, not just a few, but a couple of good, hearty laughs mixed with impromptu dance numbers to 80s music.

It is with the same carefree attitude that we invite you to roll your sleeves up, turn on the music and get your hands and kitchens dirty in making dishes that you can serve and indulge in at home or potluck parties or make in bulk, wrap creatively and give as home-made presents to loved ones. Surely, there is nothing more special than a gift borne out of your own hard labour. That's why we thank and extend our deepest appreciation to you for grabbing a copy of this, the fruit of our own hard labour. Hopefully, we have somehow made not just your Christmas but any worthwhile occasion truly special, much like the way you have made ours.

Season's Greetings and Happy Cooking!

Aileen and *Angelo*

Bottled

Flavoured Salts

Makes $1/2$ cup

3–5 tsp flavouring (e.g. chopped
    orange peel, toasted ground Sichuan
    peppercorns or dried herbs)

$1/2$ cup kosher salt

- Make sure all ingredients are dry.
- Place flavouring in a small food processor or spice grinder and process. Add salt and process until desired consistency is achieved.
- Store in a sterilised container. Keep in a cool, dark place.

Try This There are loads of ingredients you can flavour salt with.
Here are a couple of suggestions: sun-dried tomatoes, deseeded dry-roasted chillies,
dehydrated truffles and dried mushrooms.

Gift Guide Place in salt and pepper shakers. Just be sure to label them!

Depending on the flavour, this can be sprinkled on practically anything, from simple snacks like french fries to dishes such as steamed fish or risotto.

Trio of Rubs

Makes about $1/3$ cup

Spicy Steak Rub

3 dried chipotle peppers,
    deseeded, stems
    removed

2 tsp garlic powder

1 Tbsp dried oregano

2 tsp dried orange peel

2 tsp kosher salt

2 Tbsp freshly cracked
    black pepper

Herbed Chicken Rub

3 Tbsp brown sugar

2 tsp kosher salt

1 Tbsp dried basil

1 Tbsp dried oregano

$1/2$ Tbsp freshly cracked
    black pepper

1 tsp onion powder

1 tsp cayenne pepper

Citrus Fish Rub

$1^1/2$ Tbsp finely chopped
    lemon zest

$1^1/2$ Tbsp finely chopped
    orange zest

1 Tbsp garlic powder

1 tsp cayenne pepper

1 tsp kosher salt

1 tsp ground white pepper

- To prepare rubs, mix ingredients in a bowl and place in sterilised containers.
- To use, rub onto meat 10 minutes before cooking.
- Store in a cool, dry place. Use within a year.

....

Try This The recipes here are for dry rubs. Prepare wet rubs
by simply mixing dry rubs with a liquid like fruit juice or beer.

....

....

Gift Guide Keep these flavourful rubs in labelled test tubes. Stick a list of ingredients
on the test tube together with suggestions of what meats to pair the rubs with.

....

A little goes a long way,
so stash these rubs for
an instant boost of flavour.

CITRUS

HERBED

SPICY

Mediterranean Dipping Oil

Makes $1/2$ cup

Dipping Oil

$1/3$ cup olive oil

3 Tbsp balsamic vinegar

$1/2$ tsp dried chilli flakes

1 tsp dried basil

1 tsp dried oregano

$1/2$ tsp salt

$1/4$ tsp freshly cracked black pepper

- In a bowl, combine all ingredients. Mix well.
- Place in a sterilised bottle. Cover.
- Store in a cool, dry place and use within 6 months.
- To use, shake bottle until ingredients are well combined. Pour on a side plate. Sprinkle with Parmesan-Pepper.

Parmesan-Pepper

$1/2$ cup grated Parmesan cheese

$2 1/2$ tsp dried basil

1 tsp cayenne pepper

$2 1/2$ tsp freshly cracked black pepper

$1/4$ tsp salt

- In a bowl, combine all ingredients. Stir well.
- Place in a sterilised bottle. Cover.
- Store in a cool, dry place and use within 6 months.
- Use with dipping oil.

....

Try This Include other spices such as sumac or *zaatar* for a surprising twist.
Use Pecorino cheese instead of Parmesan.

....

....

Gift Guide Gift with a loaf of freshly baked focaccia (page 146)
or store-bought ciabatta in a basket together with Parmesan-Pepper.

....

The Italians always dip their breads in a mixture of olive oil and balsamic vinegar. Here's a version with herbs and spices, a flavourful recipe that serves as a dip and can also be used as a marinade for grilled or roasted poultry and pork.

Yoghurt Marinade

Makes 2 cups

2.5-cm (1-in) knob ginger, peeled

2 cloves garlic, peeled

2 cups plain yoghurt

$1^1/_2$ Tbsp garam masala

2 tsp lemon juice

$^1/_2$ tsp cayenne pepper

$^1/_2$ tsp salt

$^1/_4$ tsp freshly cracked black pepper

3 Tbsp olive oil

- Using a grater, grate ginger and garlic into a bowl.
- Add rest of ingredients, except olive oil, and mix well.
- Gently drizzle in oil while mixing.
- Taste and adjust seasoning with salt and pepper if necessary.
- Place in a sterilised container and cover.
- Store refrigerated. Use within a week.

....

Try This Use buttermilk as a substitute for yoghurt for a more tangy flavour.

....

....

Gift Guide Include a couple of nice metal or wooden skewers when giving
this marinade away. Or pair it with one of the spices used in the marinade
which your loved one might not have tried before.

....

Yoghurt does not only make for a good base for marinades, it also helps tenderise meat.

BBQ Sauce

Makes about 2^1/$_2$ cups

2 cups tomato sauce

^{1}/$_4$ cup light soy sauce

^{1}/$_4$ cup red wine vinegar

^{1}/$_4$ cup brown sugar

2 Tbsp Dijon mustard

1 Tbsp onion powder

1 Tbsp garlic powder

1 tsp hot sauce

2 tsp liquid smoke

3 Tbsp butter

- Place all ingredients, except butter, in a saucepan. Gently simmer and reduce for around 10 minutes or until desired consistency is achieved.
- Remove from heat. Add butter and mix until melted and well-incorporated.
- Pour sauce into a sterilised container. Leave to cool before covering.
- Store refrigerated. Consume within 2 months.

....

Try This Want it a tad sweeter? Add maple syrup.
For a tropical flavour, include pineapple juice in the mix.

....

....

Gift Guide Tie a basting brush to the bottle for a gift grill-lovers will truly appreciate.

....

Use this sauce to marinate
or baste meats to get that
flavourful punch.

BBQ

HAPPY
GRILLIN'
FROM Joe

Ketchup

Makes 3 cups

2 Tbsp olive oil

1 medium onion, peeled and chopped

1 medium red onion, peeled and chopped

3 Tbsp tomato paste

2 cans crushed tomatoes, each 793 g (28 oz)

1 cup dark brown sugar

$1/_2$ cup cider vinegar

1 bay leaf

$1/_2$ tsp ground cinnamon

$1/_2$ tsp ground cloves

$1/_2$ tsp ground all-spice

$1/_2$ tsp salt

$1/_4$ tsp freshly cracked black pepper

- Heat oil in a saucepan over medium heat. Add onions and sauté until softened, then add tomato paste and heat for a minute.
- Add crushed tomatoes, sugar, vinegar, bay leaf and spices. Simmer, stirring occasionally, until slightly thick, about 30 minutes.
- Remove bay leaf and purée mixture in blender until smooth. Pass through a sieve back into saucepan. Heat for another 5 minutes, stirring. Taste and adjust seasoning with salt and pepper.
- Leave to cool, then store in a sterilised container.
- Keep refrigerated. Use within 3 weeks.

....

Try This Add a kick to your ketchup by mixing in a teaspoon of hot sauce.

....

....

Gift Guide Pair a bottle of this ketchup with a bottle of mustard
and an assortment of sausages and cold cuts.

....

This popular condiment works on almost anything. It's a pantry staple anyone would find useful to receive as a home-made gift.

Caramel Sauce

Makes $2^1/_2$ cups

$1^1/_2$ cups sugar

$^1/_2$ cup water

4 Tbsp butter

1 cup double (heavy) cream

$^1/_4$ tsp salt

- Place sugar and water in a saucepan over moderate heat. Stir just once.
- Once sugar has dissolved and turned amber in colour, around 15 minutes, add butter and whisk.
- Once butter has melted and is well mixed, take pan off heat. Add cream and whisk until smooth. Be careful when handling the foam.
- Add salt and mix well. It will thicken up once cooled.
- Pour into a sterilised container and leave to cool before covering.
- Store refrigerated. Use within 2 weeks.

Tip: If the sauce ends up a bit grainy, return it to the pan and stir over low heat until smooth.

....

Try This Gently simmer for another 5 to 10 minutes for a smoother sauce.
Slightly increase quantity of salt for a salted caramel sauce.

....

....

Gift Guide Match this caramel sauce with one or a variety of sauce dishes.

....

*This is the go-to sauce to make desserts
like pies, ice creams and tarts extra special!*

Lemon Curd

Makes 3 cups

$^3/_4$ cup unsalted butter, chilled and
   cut into cubes

1 cup sugar

$^3/_4$ cup lemon juice

4 large eggs, beaten

1 tsp finely chopped lemon zest

- Place butter and sugar in a saucepan over low heat. Stir continuously.

- When sugar is melted, remove from heat. Strain in lemon juice and mix with a wooden spoon until cool.

- Add eggs and lemon zest, then return to low heat, stirring until thick, around 7 minutes.

- Strain into a sterilised container. Allow to cool completely before covering.

- Store refrigerated. Use within a week.

....

Try This Make it a complete gift by partnering the bottle of curd with kitchen items
useful for making tarts. Your baker friend will be delighted to receive it.

....

....

Gift Guide Use this recipe for making other fruit curds like orange and lime.
Just leave the zest out for non-citrus fruit like mango.

....

*Apart from using this lemon curd
to make a pie, you can use it as a spread
on cakes, scones, cupcakes or toasted bread.*

Easy Tomato Pasta Sauce

Makes 4 cups

$^1/_4$ cup olive oil

$^1/_2$ cup minced white onion

1 Tbsp minced garlic

2 Tbsp tomato paste

$^1/_2$ cup white wine

2 cans crushed tomatoes, each 793 g (28 oz)

1 Tbsp dried oregano

$^1/_2$ tsp salt

$^1/_4$ tsp freshly cracked black pepper

- Heat oil in a saucepan. Add onion and sauté until fragrant, then add garlic. Sauté lightly.
- Add tomato paste and cook for a couple of seconds.
- Pour in white wine and cook until reduced by half.
- Add tomatoes and oregano. Simmer and reduce until slightly thick.
- Season with salt and pepper.
- Transfer into a sterilised container. Leave to cool before covering.
- Store in the refrigerator for up to 1 week or in the freezer for up to 6 months.

....

Try This Use as a base for a wide range of pasta sauces such as
bolognese or creamy tomato vodka sauce.

....

....

Gift Guide Place in a basket with a packet of dry spaghetti, a chunk of hard cheese
and fresh herbs for a spaghetti-ready gift.

....

With this in stock, pasta meals can be had in mere minutes — perfect for last-minute parties.

Two Pesto Sauces

Makes 2 cups

Basil Pesto

3 cloves garlic, peeled

$^1/_4$ cup pine nuts, toasted

$^1/_2$ cup grated Parmesan cheese

$1^1/_2$ cups extra virgin olive oil + more as needed

7 cups fresh basil leaves

$^1/_2$ tsp salt

$^1/_4$ tsp freshly cracked black pepper

- Place garlic, nuts, cheese and olive oil in a food processor. Blend until smooth.
- Add basil leaves in batches. Pulse to purée. It should be slightly coarse and not smooth. Taste and adjust seasoning with salt and pepper.
- Transfer to a sterilised container. Add more olive oil to cover pesto.
- Cover and keep refrigerated. Use within 2 months.

Sun-dried Tomato Pesto

3 cups sun-dried tomatoes, drained

$^3/_4$ cup basil pesto

$^1/_4$ cup dry white wine

$^1/_2$ tsp salt

$^1/_4$ tsp freshly cracked black pepper

Extra virgin olive oil

- Rehydrate sun-dried tomatoes by soaking them in hot water. Let stand until soft. Drain. Blend in a food processor just until coarse and not smooth. Place in a bowl.
- Add basil pesto and wine. Mix well. Taste and adjust seasoning with salt and pepper.
- Transfer to a sterilised container. Add more olive oil to cover pesto.
- Cover and keep refrigerated. Use within 2 months.

Tip: The layer of oil on the pesto helps to prevent discolouration.

....

Try This Pair with breadsticks, ciabatta or pasta noodles. Or with a salad bowl. All these give hints as to what pesto is good for.

....

....

Gift Guide Want something different other than basil or sun-dried tomatoes? Try coriander leaves (cilantro), green olives or walnut pesto.

....

This classic sauce from Genoa, Italy
has many different interpretations. Here we offer
the most basic version and a most delicious one too!

Chicken Liver Pâté

Makes 3 cups

6 Tbsp butter, cut into 2.5-cm (1-in) cubes

$1/2$ cup minced white onion

1 tsp minced garlic

600 g (1 lb $5^1/3$ oz) chicken livers, trimmed and washed

2 fresh thyme leaves

2 bay leaves

$1/4$ cup brandy

1 tsp salt

$1/2$ tsp freshly cracked black pepper

Ghee (clarified butter)

- Melt butter in a large frying pan over medium heat. Add onion and cook until soft and translucent.

- Add garlic and cook until fragrant. Do not brown.

- Add chicken livers, thyme and bay leaves. Sauté lightly, then add brandy. Lower heat and simmer until livers are cooked through.

- Season with salt and pepper. Set aside to cool.

- Remove bay leaves and pour mixture into a blender. Purée until smooth. Season to taste.

- Transfer to a sterilised container and pat down. Top with a layer of ghee.

- Cover and chill before serving.

- Store refrigerated. Use within 3 days of opening.

....

Try This Sauté the onions with a little chopped bacon for a richer flavour.

....

....

Gift Guide Dress up a plain-looking container or give away with a pack of Melba toast and a butter knife to make for a complete appetiser gift.

....

*Rich in flavour and very easy to make,
this is great to have on standby
for when unexpected guests drop in.*

Flavoured Vinegar

Makes 3 cups

8 sprigs fresh rosemary

8 sprigs fresh thyme

3 cups red wine vinegar

10 cloves garlic, peeled

- Rinse fresh herbs and pat dry. Make sure there is no trace of moisture or bacteria may grow.

- Gently insert herbs inside a clean bottle, filling it to around one-third to half full.

- Simmer vinegar in a saucepan until it is close to boiling. Pour inside herb-stuffed bottle. Leave to cool before covering.

- Refrigerate for a week to a month. Then, using a coffee filter, strain vinegar until it is no longer cloudy.

- Pour into a sterilised bottle and use within 3 months.

....

Try This Other flavour combinations are lemon and strawberries for cider vinegar, garlic and basil for white wine vinegar, and lime and chillies for white vinegar.

....

....

Gift Guide Make sure to attach a note indicating the date the vinegar was made and the consume-by date.

....

Use this to deglaze pans or dress salads.
Or use as a condiment for calamari,
fish and chips or grilled meats.

Olive Tapenade

Makes 1$^1/_2$ cups

3 cups pitted Kalamata olives, chopped

1 cup pitted green olives, chopped

4 Tbsp capers, drained

2 tsp lemon juice

2 anchovy fillets

4 cloves garlic, peeled and finely chopped

$^1/_2$ cup parsley leaves, chopped

$^2/_3$ cup extra virgin olive oil

$^1/_2$ tsp salt

$^1/_4$ tsp freshly cracked black pepper

- Place olives, capers, lemon juice, anchovies, garlic and parsley in a food processor. Pulse a couple of times until it forms a coarse paste.
- Gently drizzle in olive oil while pulsing. Make sure to still retain some texture by not puréeing the olives too much.
- Taste and adjust seasoning with salt and pepper.
- Place in a sterilised container and cover.
- Store refrigerated. Use within 2 weeks.

....

Try This Use your choice of olives or a combination of three or more types of olives.

....

....

Gift Guide Include a card listing down the many uses of olive tapenade and give it away with a loaf of bread or a bag of crostini.

....

This Provençal dish, typically served as an appetiser spread on bread or toast, is also the filling we used for the olive palmiers (page 118). This can also be tossed with pasta for a vegetarian treat.

Smoked Salmon Spread

Makes $3/4$ cup

$1/2$ cup cream cheese, softened

2 Tbsp sour cream

1 tsp lemon juice

1 tsp lemon zest

1 Tbsp minced onion

1 Tbsp capers, minced

$1/2$ Tbsp minced parsley

$1/8$ tsp salt

$1/8$ tsp freshly cracked black pepper

2 Tbsp chopped smoked salmon

- Using a food processor, whip cream cheese until smooth and creamy. Add sour cream, lemon juice and zest. Whip until well combined.

- Add onion, capers and parsley. Whip until well combined.

- Season with salt and pepper.

- Add smoked salmon. Pulse 2 to 3 times or just until combined.

- Place in a sterilised container and cover.

- Store refrigerated. Use within 4 days.

....

Try This Add chopped dill for an additional layer of flavour to complement smoked salmon.

....
....

Gift Guide Place in hand-painted ceramic bowls for a personal touch.

....

Elicit compliments from your guests with this simple appetiser. Match with neutral flavoured crackers so the taste of smoked salmon can shine through.

Chilli Jam

Makes 3 cups

6 bird's eye chillies, roughly chopped

5-cm (2-in) knob ginger, peeled and
    roughly chopped

6 cloves garlic, peeled

2 cans crushed tomatoes, each 400 g
    (14$^1/_3$ oz)

2 cups sugar

$^2/_3$ cup cider vinegar

2 tsp lemon juice

- Place chillies, ginger and garlic in a food processor and process into a purée.

- Add crushed tomatoes and process until smooth.

- Place purée in a pan along with sugar, vinegar and lemon juice. Bring to the boil, then lower heat and reduce to a simmer until slightly thick, around 50 minutes, stirring occasionally.

- Pour into a sterilised container. Leave to cool before covering.

- Store refrigerated. Use within 3 months.

Try This Play around with various types of chillies that you can find to spike up the flavour.

Gift Guide Place in a wok or basket along with other stir-fry ingredients with a recipe card to guide your loved ones on how to use the jam.

*This sweet and spicy condiment is great
on practically anything, from sandwiches to stir-fries.*

Chunky Mango-Lemon Chutney

Makes 3$\frac{1}{2}$ cups

1 cup sugar

1 cup white wine vinegar

$\frac{1}{2}$ tsp chilli flakes

$\frac{1}{2}$ tsp ground ginger

$\frac{1}{2}$ tsp onion powder

5 medium-size ripe mangoes, peeled
   and cut into cubes

$\frac{1}{3}$ cup raisins

1 Tbsp minced preserved lemon
   (optional)

2 Tbsp lemon juice

- Place sugar and vinegar in a pot over medium heat. Simmer, stirring until sugar is dissolved.

- Add chilli flakes, ground ginger and onion powder and mix.

- Put in two-thirds of mango cubes, raisins, preserved lemon and lemon juice. Simmer for 30 minutes, then add remainder of mangoes. Continue simmering until mixture is thick, stirring occasionally.

- Remove from heat and leave to cool. Transfer into sterilised containers and cover.

- Store refrigerated. Use within 3 weeks.

....

Try This Mango isn't the only item you can turn into chutneys.
Try using apples, pears, cranberries, ginger and tomatoes!

....

....

Gift Guide Place chutney, frozen roti and some tandoori mix in a basket
for an Indian-inspired meal.

....

This delightful side dish is a perfect accompaniment to Indian and other spicy dishes.

Marinated Feta

Serves 4 to 6

400 g (14^1/$_3$ oz) feta cheese, cut into cubes

1 tsp dried rosemary

1^1/$_2$ tsp freshly cracked black pepper

1^1/$_2$ tsp chilli flakes

2 Tbsp lemon juice

2 cups extra virgin olive oil + more
as needed

- Arrange cubed feta cheese in a sterilised jar.
- In a bowl, mix rosemary, black pepper, chilli flakes, lemon juice and olive oil. Pour over feta.
- Add more olive oil as needed to fully cover cheese.
- Cover with lid and leave to marinate for at least 24 hours for flavours to meld.
- Store refrigerated. Use within 2 weeks.

....

Try This You can opt to marinate other cheeses such as manchego or goat's cheese.

....

....

Gift Guide Is your loved one a cheese lover too?
Pair a jar of feta with a book on cheeses or a recipe book on appetisers.

....

Include this in salads, use as a topping over pizza or simply spread over crackers for another dimension of flavour.

TO Aidan

Marinated Olives

Serves 6 to 8

1 Tbsp dried oregano

1 Tbsp dried thyme

1 cup extra virgin olive oil

$^1/_2$ cup red wine vinegar

4 cups pitted black and green olives

- Mix dried herbs, olive oil and red wine vinegar together.
- Add olives and toss well.
- Place in a sterilised container. Cover and leave to marinate for at least 24 hours before using.
- Store refrigerated. Use within 2 weeks.

....

Try This Use olives of your choice. Add anchovy fillets and red pimiento for more stuff to snack on.

....

....

Gift Guide Cover the jar with a pretty piece of cloth and tie with a ribbon.

....

This Italian antipasto is so easy to make for giving away whatever the occasion. The longer you leave the olives in the marinade, the better it tastes.

Lemon-Garlic Oil

Makes 2 cups

1 tsp whole black peppercorns

5 cloves garlic, peeled

Lemon zest from 1 lemon, sliced

2 cups olive oil

- Place peppercorns, garlic and lemon zest in a sterilised container. Fill the container with olive oil.

- Cover and refrigerate for 2 days before using.

- Store refrigerated. Use within a week.

Tip: When using fresh ingredients like fresh herbs, fruit peels and chillies or peppers, use them dry and consume the flavoured oil within a week to make sure no bacteria develops. Also, be sure to keep the flavoured oils refrigerated as they do not keep well at room temperature.

....

Try This There are tons of other herbs and flavourings to choose from. When flavouring olive oil which has a very strong taste, use basil, tarragon, oregano and parsley. If you want the flavour of the herbs to be more pronounced, use mint, ginger and chilli with canola oil.

....

....

Gift Guide Attach a "consume before" note to the jar, and while you're at it, include a list of dishes where this can be drizzled on: pastas, salads or any savoury dish that uses oil.

....

*Use this flavoured oil to finish off
a seared chicken or a fish dish
or cooked pasta.*

Merry
Christmas

Raspberry Vinaigrette

Makes 1 cup

$^1/_4$ cup frozen raspberries

2 Tbsp water

2 Tbsp sugar

2 Tbsp red wine vinegar

1 tsp Dijon mustard

1 Tbsp minced shallots

$^1/_4$ tsp salt

$^1/_4$ tsp freshly cracked black pepper

$^1/_2$ cup extra virgin olive oil

- Place raspberries, water and sugar in a saucepan over low heat. Simmer until sugar is dissolved, takes 3 to 5 minutes. Purée mixture in a blender.

- Combine raspberry purée and remaining ingredients in a bowl. Whisk together until well mixed.

- Taste and adjust seasoning with more salt and pepper if necessary.

- Pour into a sterilised container and cover.

- Store refrigerated. Use within a week.

....

Try This Use fresh raspberries if available. You may substitute with strawberries as well.

....

....

Gift Guide Use beautiful bottles from store-bought condiments.
Once you've used up the contents, sterilise the bottles for storing vinaigrette.

....

There is nothing much to this, really.
Just process, mix and enjoy.
It is good on nutty and fruity salads.

Orange-Tarragon Vinaigrette

Makes 1 cup

$1/3$ cup freshly squeezed orange juice

1 Tbsp orange zest

2 Tbsp sugar

2 Tbsp red wine vinegar

1 tsp Dijon mustard

1 Tbsp chopped tarragon leaves

1 Tbsp minced shallots

$1/4$ tsp salt

$1/4$ tsp freshly cracked black pepper

$1/2$ cup extra virgin olive oil

- Combine everything in a bowl. Whisk together until well mixed.
- Taste and adjust seasoning if necessary.
- Pour into a sterilised container and cover.
- Store refrigerated.

....

Try This Replace tarragon with ginger for a unique flavour profile.

....

....

Gift Guide Print the recipe and paste it on the bottle. This will allow your loved one to prepare more of the dressing even after the gift has been used up.

....

Making this is as easy as putting all the ingredients in a jar, sealing it with a lid and shaking it. This doubles as an oil-based salad dressing and a citrus marinade.

Grilled Vegetable Antipasto

Serves 4 to 6

1 cup extra virgin olive oil

$^1/_4$ cup red wine vinegar

1 tsp honey

1 tsp dried oregano

$^1/_2$ tsp salt

$^1/_4$ tsp freshly cracked black pepper

1 large red capsicum (bell pepper)

1 large green capsicum (bell pepper)

1 large yellow capsicum (bell pepper)

2 large white onions, peeled and cut
  into 2.5-cm (1-in) thick rounds

3 aubergines (eggplants/brinjals), cut
  lengthwise into 1-cm ($^1/_2$-in) slices

- Combine extra virgin olive oil, vinegar, honey, oregano, salt, and black pepper in a bowl. Set aside.

- Roast capsicums over an open flame, turning frequently until charred. Put immediately into a plastic bag and seal. Leave for 10 minutes, then peel. Remove stem, seeds and ribs and cut into quarters. Set aside.

- Arrange onions and aubergines in a deep dish and pour oil mixture over. Cover and leave to marinate for at least 10 minutes. Turn onions and aubergines over after 5 minutes.

- Grill onion and aubergines until marked and cooked through. Arrange in a sterilised container along with capsicums and pour in remaining marinade.

- Cover and store refrigerated. Use within 2 weeks.

....

Try This Grill tomatoes, mushrooms, broccoli, asparagus and
courgettes (zucchinis) as well and include in the mix.

....

....

Gift Guide Include a bottle of the marinade along with the antipasto
so your loved one can use it to baste the veggies before serving.

....

Served before the meal (the literal meaning of antipasto),
this quick and easy dish gets much of its flavour from the grill.
It is a starter that can hold its own beside any main course.

Granola

Makes 4 cups

2 cups rolled oats

$^1/_2$ cup sliced almonds

$^1/_2$ cup desiccated coconut

$^1/_4$ cup raisins

$^1/_4$ cup dried cranberries

$^1/_4$ cup light brown sugar

$^1/_4$ tsp salt

$^1/_2$ tsp ground cinnamon

2 Tbsp vegetable oil

3 Tbsp honey

1 Tbsp maple syrup

- Preheat oven to 150°C (300°F). Line a baking tray with parchment paper.
- Place oats, almonds, desiccated coconut, raisins, cranberries, sugar, salt and cinnamon in a bowl. Mix well and set aside.
- Combine vegetable oil, honey and maple syrup in another bowl. Mix until well combined. Pour over oat mixture. Toss well.
- Spread oat mixture over prepared baking tray and bake for 30 minutes. Stir occasionally.
- Leave granola to cool before transferring to a sterilised airtight container.
- Store in a cool, dry place. Use within 6 months.

....

Try This Add more texture and flavour to the mix with other kinds of nuts like cashews and walnuts. You can also include sesame seeds or sunflower seeds.

....

....

Gift Guide Store in a decorative milk bottle or bowl. Great for mornings when breakfast is in a rush.

....

Perk up your mornings and snack times by sprinkling
this over yoghurt and fresh fruit, or enjoy with milk
just as you would cereal.

Preserved Lemons

Makes 7

7 lemons

7 Tbsp kosher salt + more as needed

Lemon juice

- Lightly scrub, wash and pat dry lemons. Slice off stem tip of each lemon, then cut into quarters, but do not cut all the way through. Keep lemons attached at the base.

- Spoon 1 Tbsp salt into each lemon, then reshape.

- Place a thin layer of salt at the bottom of a sterilised jar. Place lemons in the jar, pushing down firmly to extract some juice. Sprinkle more salt over lemons before replacing lid on jar.

- Leave at room temperature for a few days and shake every now and then to distribute the salt and juice. If, after 2 days, the lemons are not submerged in their own juice, add lemon juice to cover lemons.

- These preserved lemons will be ready for use after a month. Store refrigerated. Use within 6 months.

- To use, rinse off salt, remove pulp and slice peel according to desired size and shape.

....

Try This Add a hint of flavour by putting in spices like cinnamon quill, cloves, peppercorns or bay leaf.

....

....

Gift Guide Attach a recipe for chicken tagine or other dishes this can be good for. Preserved lemons can be used to flavour butter, seasoned rubs or beurre blanc sauce and prepare lamb and chicken stews.

....

A staple in many
Moroccan dishes, these are
basically lemons pickled in
salt and their own juices.

Orange-Berry Vodka

Makes 2$^1/_2$ cups

1 cup cranberry juice
1 cup orange juice
$^1/_2$ cup vodka
Lemon wedges

- Mix juices and vodka together in a pitcher.

- Transfer to a sterilised container. Cover and cool.

- Store refrigerated. Use within a week.

- Serve with lemon wedges.

··

Try This Flavour your drink accessories by using citrus fruit stirrers or mint ice cubes.
Or add spice and zing to your rim by adding flavour to the salt. Want a bolder red colour
to match the season? Simply add grenadine.

··

··

Gift Guide Make this extra special by bundling it with a cocktail shaker.

··

Get the party started with less than five ingredients!
Have family and friends toasting to this cocktail
which can be done in one easy step!

Boxed

Rugelach

Makes 16 pieces

$^1/_3$ cup butter

2 Tbsp shortening

$^1/_4$ cup cream cheese

2 Tbsp sugar

$^1/_4$ tsp salt

2$^1/_4$ cups plain (all-purpose) flour

1 large egg

1 tsp water

$^1/_2$ cup walnuts, chopped

$^1/_4$ cup brown sugar + more for topping

- Place butter, shortening, cream cheese, sugar and salt in a food processor. Pulse several times until well combined. Add flour and pulse just until mixture forms a dough.

- Remove dough from processor and roll into a ball. Flatten into a disc and cover with plastic wrap. Refrigerate until firm, at least 2 hours. (This dough can be kept frozen for up to 3 months. Thaw before using.)

- Preheat oven to 180°C (350°F). Line a baking tray with parchment paper or silicon mat.

- In a small bowl, combine egg with 1 tsp water to make an egg wash. Set aside.

- Place chilled dough between 2 sheets of parchment paper and roll out into a 28-cm (11-in) diameter circle, about 0.5-cm ($^1/_4$-in) thick, dusting lightly with flour as needed.

- Cut around dough using a dinner plate as a guide to make a perfect circle. Trim off and discard scraps.

- Brush dough circle with egg wash. Sprinkle with walnuts and brown sugar.

- Using a sharp knife or pizza cutter, cut circle into 16 equal wedges. Starting from the wide end, rolling up each wedge of dough.

- Place on prepared baking trays, seam side down. Brush rolls with egg wash and sprinkle with brown sugar.

- Bake for 30 to 32 minutes or until pastry is golden brown. Transfer to a wire rack to cool completely.

- Store in an airtight container. Keep in a cool, dry place. Consume within 4 days.

Try This Add more texture by rolling the pastry in chopped nuts, raisins and preserves before baking.

Gift Guide Wrap rugelach individually in multi-coloured cellophane and place in a clear container.

These crescent-shaped pastries look like mini croissants. Rugelach literally means little twists in Yiddish.

Jam Thumbprints

Makes about 48 cookies

$^2/_3$ cup butter, cut into cubes and softened

$^1/_3$ cup sugar

1 large egg

$1^1/_2$ cups plain (all-purpose) flour

$^1/_2$ cup strawberry jam

- Preheat oven to 180°C (350°F). Line 2 to 3 baking trays with parchment or silicon mats. Set aside.

- Using an electric mixer, beat butter and sugar until light and fluffy.

- Add egg and beat until well combined.

- Reduce speed to low. Add flour and mix just until incorporated.

- Scoop dough into $^1/_2$ Tbsp portions and shape into balls about 2.5-cm (1-in) in diameter. Place on prepared baking trays, keeping them at least 8-cm (3-in) apart.

- Moisten your thumb with water, then gently press the centre of each ball, making an indentation 1-cm ($^1/_2$-in) wide and 0.5-cm ($^1/_4$-in) deep. Alternatively, use a flower-shaped mould to create the indentation.

- Place jam in a saucepan and heat until liquefied.

- Spoon about $^1/_2$ tsp jam into each indentation.

- Bake cookies for 18 to 20 minutes or until cookies are golden brown around the edges.

- Transfer to a wire rack and allow to cool completely.

- Store in an airtight container. Keep in a cool, dry place. Consume within 3 days.

....

Try This Turn everybody's favourite peanut butter into a thumbprint cookie.
Just add peanut butter to the dough in this recipe.

....

....

Gift Guide Pack two different jam-flavoured thumbprints and gift with a checkerboard.
Use these thumbprint cookies as pawns that kids can play with and eat after.

....

Here is a tea cookie that even kids can help to make.
You may shape the cookies into balls, then use your thumb
to press on the cookies or use a cookie mould for a prettier presentation.

Apricot Macadamia Brownies

Makes one 30 x 20-cm (12 x 8-in) cake

$^2/_3$ cup butter, cut into cubes

$1^2/_3$ cups brown sugar

3 large eggs

1 tsp vanilla extract

2 Tbsp light corn syrup

$1^1/_3$ cups plain (all-purpose) flour

$^1/_2$ tsp baking soda

$^1/_2$ tsp salt

$^2/_3$ cups dried apricots, chopped

$^1/_2$ cup macadamia nuts, chopped

- Preheat oven to 180°F (350°F). Lightly grease a 30 x 20-cm (12 x 8-in) baking pan. Set aside.

- In a medium saucepan, melt butter over low heat. Add brown sugar and mix until combined. Remove from heat.

- Add eggs one at a time, beating well after each addition. Mix in vanilla extract and light corn syrup.

- In a separate bowl, whisk together flour, baking soda and salt. Gradually add to butter mixture, mixing just until combined. Do not over mix or batter will become tough.

- Add apricots and nuts. Stir well.

- Transfer batter to prepared pan.

- Bake for 23 to 25 minutes or until a cake tester inserted into the centre of cake comes out clean but not dry.

- Cool completely before slicing. Store refrigerated. Consume within a week.

....

Try This Make these brownies more of a treat by adding chocolate chips
along with the nuts and dried fruit.

....

....

Gift Guide Leave the cake whole, cover with cellophane and place on a serving tray or wooden box.

....

Give this all-time favourite a twist by throwing in
a different kind of nut from the usual and adding dried fruit.

Date & Nut Tassies

Makes 24 mini pies

$^2/_3$ cup butter, cut into cubes and softened

$^1/_4$ cup shortening

$^1/_2$ cup cream cheese, cut into cubes and softened

$^1/_4$ cup sugar

$^1/_2$ tsp salt

2 cups plain (all-purpose) flour

$^1/_4$ cup bittersweet chocolate, melted

Filling

1 large egg

$^3/_4$ cup brown sugar

2 Tbsp melted butter

$^1/_2$ cup dates, chopped

$^1/_2$ cup walnuts, chopped

- Preheat oven to 160°C (325°F). Prepare 2 to 3 muffin trays with 4.5-cm ($1^3/_4$-in) diameter cups. You will need a total of 24 cups. Set aside.

- Using an electric mixer fitted with a paddle attachment, beat butter, shortening and cream cheese on medium speed until just well combined.

- Reduce speed to low and gradually stir in sugar, salt and flour.

- Scoop dough into 1 Tbsp rounds and gently press into the bottom and sides of muffin cups. Set aside.

- Prepare filling. In a small bowl, combine egg, brown sugar and butter. Stir until well combined, then stir in dates and walnuts.

- Spoon about 1 tsp filling into each pastry-lined muffin cup. Bake for 25 to 30 minutes or until pastry is golden and filling is puffed.

- Remove from oven and leave to cool completely.

- Drizzle with melted chocolate before serving.

- Store in an airtight container. Keep in a cool, dry place. Consume within 4 days.

....

Try This Use an assortment of nuts instead of just one kind.

....
....

Gift Guide Wrap individually in different coloured cellophane and place in a decorative basket or tin can.

....

Tassies are like baby pecan pies.
We put a twist to these babies by using
dates and walnuts which make them
more chewy and gooey.

Lamingtons

Makes 48 squares

1 cup butter, cut into cubes and
  softened

1^2/$_3$ cups sugar

4 large eggs

1 Tbsp vanilla extract

3 cups cake flour

1^1/$_4$ Tbsp baking powder

^{1}/$_2$ cup salt

1^1/$_3$ cups milk

2 cups flaked coconut

Glaze

2 cups icing (confectioner's) sugar

^{1}/$_4$ cup milk

2 Tbsp butter

- Preheat oven to 180°C (350°F). Line and grease a 32 x 24-cm (12 x 9-in) baking pan. Set aside.

- Using an electric mixer, beat butter and sugar until light and fluffy.

- Add eggs one at a time, beating each egg for about 1 minute.

- Add vanilla extract and continue beating until combined.

- In a separate bowl, sift together flour, baking powder and salt. Add a third of flour to butter mixture, then half the milk. Beat until combined. Repeat process until flour and milk are incorporated.

- Pour batter into prepared pan. Bake for 30 to 35 minutes or until a cake tester inserted into the centre of cake comes out clean. Transfer cake to a wire rack to cool completely before cutting into 4-cm (1^1/$_2$-in) squares.

- Prepare glaze. Using an electric mixer, mix icing sugar and milk until smooth. Add butter and mix well. Transfer to a bowl.

- Dip cake in glaze and ensure all sides are evenly coated. Roll and dredge cake in flaked coconut before serving.

- Store in an airtight container. Keep refrigerated. Consume within 4 days.

Try This Add a little red or green food colouring to the glaze to make lamingtons colourful.

Gift Guide Stack cubes on a plate to form a Christmas tree.

These mini sponge cakes are originally dipped in a chocolate glaze and rolled in coconut flakes. Omitting the chocolate dip makes them look like little cakes in the snow, keeping up with the holiday theme.

Alfajores

Makes about 24 sandwich cookies

1 cup butter, cut into cubes and softened

$^1/_2$ cup sugar

1 tsp vanilla extract

$1^1/_2$ cups plain (all-purpose) flour

$^1/_3$ cup rice flour

$^1/_4$ tsp salt

1 cup icing (confectioner's) sugar

2 cans sweetened condensed milk,
    each 396 g (14 oz)

- Line 2 to 3 baking trays with greased parchment paper or silicon mats. Set aside.
- Using an electric mixer, beat butter and sugar until light and fluffy. Add vanilla extract and mix well.
- In a separate bowl, whisk together flours and salt.
- Gradually add flours and mix into a dough. Cover dough with plastic wrap and chill for at least 30 minutes.
- Preheat oven to 160°C (325°F).
- Roll chilled dough between sheets of plastic wrap or parchment paper to 0.2-cm ($^1/_8$-in) thickness. Cut out dough into 4-cm ($1^1/_2$-in) diameter rounds. You should get about 48 rounds. Place rounds on prepared baking trays.
- Bake for 15 to 20 minutes or until cookies are slightly golden around the edges.
- Leave to cool completely before dusting with icing sugar. Store in an airtight container.
- Prepare toffee. Remove paper label from cans of condensed milk. Fill a medium saucepan with water and bring to the boil. Lower heat to low and keep water at a gentle simmer. Submerge cans in water and allow to simmer for 2 hours. Top up with water as needed to keep cans completely submerged in water.
- Remove cans from water. Allow to cool at room temperature before opening. Takes about 2 hours. Place toffee in an airtight container and keep refrigerated until ready to use.
- To assemble, spoon toffee into a piping bag fitted with a round tip. Pipe 1 to 2 tsp toffee on the flat side of a cookie, then sandwich with another cookie. Repeat until ingredients are used up.
- Wrap cookies individually in cellophane or greaseproof paper.
- Store in an airtight container. Keep refrigerated. Consume within a week.

Try This Give these cookies some zing by adding lemon and orange zest to the dough.

Gift Guide Stack these cookies in a cookie jar and tie with a bow.

These traditional Spanish sandwich cookies typically flavoured with cinnamon make for a perfect Christmas meal ender.

Coconut Macaroons

Makes about 20 macaroons

3 cups dried unsweetened shredded coconut

$^1/_8$ tsp salt

$^2/_3$ cup sweetened condensed milk

1 Tbsp coconut extract

Egg whites from 2 large eggs

$^1/_2$ cup dark coating chocolate, melted

- Combine shredded coconut, salt, condensed milk, coconut extract and egg whites in a bowl. Mix well.

- Refrigerate for at least 1 hour or until firm to the touch.

- Preheat oven to 160°C (325°F). Line baking trays with parchment paper or silicon mats. Set aside.

- Scoop about 1 Tbsp mixture and shape into a cone. Repeat until ingredients are used up. Wet hands if mixture becomes too sticky to handle.

- Place cones on prepared trays, spacing them 5-cm (2-in) apart.

- Bake for 18 to 20 minutes or until edges of macaroons are dry and golden. Leave to cool completely on wire racks.

- Finish off macaroons by dipping bottoms in melted chocolate. Place on same lined baking trays. Allow chocolate to dry completely.

- Store in airtight containers. Keep in a cool, dry place. Consume within 3 days.

....

Try This Add nuts like almonds, pecans and cashews to these coconut macaroons. Or put jam in the middle of it.

....

....

Gift Guide Place in small fish bowls or glass vases to make them easier to grab and pop in the mouth.

....

Chewy on the outside and soft on the inside,
these cookies are one of the easiest to make
and among the most pleasurable to eat.

Champagne Truffles

Makes 24

350 g (12 oz) dark coating chocolate, melted
1 cup cocoa powder

Ganache
1 cup double (heavy) cream
450 g (1 lb) dark chocolate, chopped
2 Tbsp butter
$^1/_3$ cup brandy or as desired

- Line 2 to 3 baking trays with greased parchment paper or silicon mats. Set aside.

- Prepare ganache. Bring cream to the boil in a saucepan, then turn off heat. Stir in chocolate until melted and smooth. Stir in butter, followed by brandy.

- Transfer mixture to a bowl. Refrigerate for at least 1 hour or until ganache is firm.

- Scoop ganache into 2.5-cm (1-in) diameter balls. Roll each portion by hand. Place on prepared trays and refrigerate for at least 1 hour.

- Dip ganache balls in melted coating chocolate using a fork, then immediately roll in cocoa powder to get a hard crust and a soft centre.

- Leave to set completely on prepared baking trays.

- Place truffles in truffle cups. Store in an airtight container at cool room temperature. Consume within 2 weeks.

....

Try This Use other flavourings in place of brandy. Try Grand Marnier, amaretto, hazelnut or coffee. Roll in white and milk chocolate shavings or hide a piece of marshmallow in the middle of the ganache.

....
....

Gift Guide Place in vintage tin boxes or pair with a bottle of bubbly for a nice night-capper.

....

It's hard not to sneak a mouthful of these when you know they're made with chocolate and liquor.

Whisky Brownies

Makes 18 bars

1 cup unsweetened chocolate, chopped

1 cup butter, cut into cubes

$1^2/_3$ cups sugar

4 large eggs

1 tsp vanilla extract

1 cup plain (all-purpose) flour

$^1/_4$ tsp salt

3 Tbsp whisky

Glaze

$^1/_2$ cup whipping cream or double (heavy) cream

1 cup bittersweet chocolate, chopped

2 Tbsp whisky

- Preheat oven to 180°C (350°F). Lightly grease a 23-cm (9-in) square baking pan.

- In a medium bowl set over a pot of simmering water, combine chocolate and butter, stirring occasionally until completely melted. Remove from heat.

- Whisk sugar in chocolate mixture. Whisk in eggs one at a time, then add in vanilla extract.

- Gradually add in flour and salt, mixing until smooth. Transfer batter into prepared pan.

- Bake for 30 to 35 minutes or until a cake tester inserted into the centre of cake comes out slightly moist. Do not over bake.

- Remove from oven, brush the top with 3 Tbsp whisky and leave to cool completely on a wire rack.

- Prepare glaze. Boil cream in a small saucepan and pour over chocolate. Stir until chocolate is melted and smooth. Add whisky and stir until smooth.

- Spread glaze evenly over brownies. Slice into 18 bars, each about 7.5 x 4-cm (3 x $1^1/_2$-in) to serve.

- Store refrigerated. Consume within 4 days.

....

Try This Replace whisky with your liquor of choice.

....

....

Gift Guide Pack these brownies with a bag of good coffee.

....

Of the countless kinds of brownies
that have already been made and remade,
we guarantee that this is one version
that will leave you in high spirits. Cheers!

Chocolate Mint Cupcakes

Makes 18 cupcakes

1^1/$_3$ cups plain (all-purpose) flour

1 cup cocoa powder

1^1/$_3$ cups sugar

2 tsp baking powder

^{1}/$_2$ tsp baking soda

^{1}/$_2$ tsp salt

^{2}/$_3$ cup cooking oil

2 large eggs

^{1}/$_4$ cup milk

1 tsp vanilla extract

1 cup boiling water

Red and silver dragées

Icing

1 cup egg whites

1^1/$_2$ cups sugar

1–2 drops peppermint oil

- Preheat oven to 180°C (350°F). Line two 12-hole muffin pans with paper liners.

- In a bowl, whisk together flour, cocoa powder, sugar, baking powder, baking soda and salt.

- In another bowl, whisk together oil, eggs, milk and vanilla extract. Mix well.

- Using an electric mixer, gradually add liquid mixture to dry mixture, beating on medium speed until combined. Add boiling water and beat for another minute.

- Fill lined pans with batter to about three-quarters full. Bake for 25 to 30 minutes or until a cake tester inserted into the centre of cake comes out clean. Remove cupcakes from the oven, then transfer to a wire rack to cool completely before frosting.

- To make icing, place egg whites and sugar into the bowl of an electric mixer. Place bowl over a saucepan of simmering water. Stir mixture with a wire whisk until sugar is dissolved and mixture is warm to the touch. Remove bowl from the pan and whisk mixture on high speed until stiff and shiny peaks form.

- Spoon mixture into a piping bag fitted with a large round tip (no. 807). Pipe icing in a spiral upward motion starting from the edge of a cupcake and going up towards the middle to form an inverted cone. Repeat to ice all cupcakes. Decorate with dragées.

- Store refrigerated. Consume within 3 days.

Try This Colour the icing and use different-coloured dragées and sprinkles.

Gift Guide Place individually in cupcake boxes and tie with a bow. Give as a door gift or party favour.

These look like plain chocolate cupcakes
but once you bite into them, the minty flavor
will be a most welcome surprise!

Cheese Torta

Makes one 7.5-cm (3-in) diameter torta

1 Tbsp olive oil

1 Tbsp minced onion

1 tsp minced garlic

$^2/_3$ cup cream cheese, softened

1 Tbsp parsley

$^1/_4$ tsp chopped fresh thyme

$^1/_4$ tsp salt

$^1/_8$ tsp freshly cracked black pepper

$1^1/_2$ Tbsp basil pesto (page 34)

$1^1/_2$ Tbsp sun-dried tomato pesto (page 34)

- Line the side of a 7.5-cm (3-in) diameter ring mould with acetate. Place mould on a small cake board.

- Heat olive oil in a small frying pan and sauté onion, then garlic. Cook until fragrant. Set aside to cool completely.

- Place cream cheese, parsley and thyme into a food processor with cooled onion and garlic. Process until smooth. Season with salt and pepper to taste.

- Divide mixture into 3 equal portions.

- Spoon a portion into prepared mould. Level it, then top with basil pesto. Spread evenly. Spoon another portion of cream cheese mixture over. Spread evenly. Top with sun-dried tomato pesto. Finish with the last portion of cream cheese mixture. Spread evenly to level off the top.

- Refrigerate for at least 1 hour or overnight to set.

- Store refrigerated. Consume within 4 days.

....

Try This In keeping with the red-white-and-green theme, you can opt to use goat's cheese, roasted peppers and green olive tapenade.

....

....

Gift Guide Place in wide glass containers so your loved ones can enjoy the look and colours as soon as they receive the gift.

....

It's festive, both in colour and taste.
Serve this appetiser with crackers and flatbreads.

Caviar Pie

Makes one 15-cm (6-in) pie

$^1/_2$ cup cream cheese, softened

2 Tbsp sour cream

2 Tbsp minced onion

2 Tbsp minced chives

2 Tbsp minced hard-boiled eggs

3–4 Tbsp caviar

- Line the side of a 7.5-cm (3-in) diameter ring mould with acetate. Place mould on a small cake board.

- Using a food processor, whip cream cheese until smooth and creamy. Add sour cream and whip until fluffy. Spoon mixture into prepared mould.

- Spoon chopped onion over cream cheese mixture. Level off using a spatula or spoon.

- Sprinkle chives evenly on top, then spread chopped egg evenly over chives. Spoon caviar on top.

- Leave to set in the refrigerator for at least 3 hours or overnight.

- To serve, unmould pie onto a serving plate. Serve with crostini or crackers.

- Store refrigerated. Consume within 4 days.

....

Try This Use inexpensive caviar like salmon, whitefish or lumpfish.
Create edible art by using two kinds of caviar in different colours.

....

....

Gift Guide Give away on a nice serving plate, surrounded by crostini or crackers.

....

It's not really a pie encased in a flaky shell
but more of a layered spread. Once you get a taste of this,
you simply won't be able to get enough of it.

Ensaymada

Makes 12 buns

1 Tbsp active dry yeast

$^1/_2$ cup warm water

$3^1/_3$ cups plain (all-purpose) flour

$^1/_2$ cup sugar

1 tsp salt

8 large eggs

$^1/_3$ cup milk

$^1/_2$ cup butter, softened + more
   for brushing

Topping

$^1/_2$ cup butter, cut into cubes and
   softened

1 cup sugar

1 cup cheddar cheese

- In the bowl of an electric mixer, dissolve yeast in warm water. Stir and leave for about 5 minutes until bubbly.

- In a separate bowl, sift together flour, sugar and salt.

- Using an electric mixer fitted with a dough hook, gradually add flour mixture to activated yeast on low speed.

- Mix in eggs and milk and knead until dough is smooth and elastic. Takes 15 to 20 minutes. Transfer dough onto a greased work surface.

- Roll dough into a log. Divide into 12 equal portions, each weighing about 65 g ($2^1/_3$ oz). Roll each portion of dough into a smooth ball. Flatten with a rolling pin until about 0.5-cm ($^1/_4$-in) thick, 18-cm (7-in) long and 7.5-cm (3-in) wide.

- Brush dough generously with butter. Starting from a long edge, roll dough into a long rope. Twist rope, then form into a knot and tuck loose ends in at the bottom of dough. Repeat with remaining dough.

- Place shaped dough into ensaymada moulds. Brioche moulds or fluted/scalloped moulds will do as well. Leave to rise for 1 hour or until double in size.

- Preheat oven to 150°C (300°F). Bake buns for 12 to 15 minutes. Leave to cool.

- Prepare topping. Using an electric mixer, cream butter and sugar until light and fluffy, take about 5 minutes.

- Spread about $^1/_2$ Tbsp topping on each bun. Top with grated cheese.

- Wrap buns with clear plastic sheets or parchment paper.

- Store refrigerated for up to 6 days. Keep frozen for longer shelf life.

Try This Top these delicate pastries with Parmesan cheese or gouda for a richer flavour.

Gift Guide Pair these pastries with a bag of hot cocoa mix or chocolate blocks/tablets and a recipe for hot chocolate.

*These brioche-type pastries
are tender, moist, buttery and cheesy.
They are best eaten warm with a mug of
thick Spanish hot chocolate.*

Taisan

Makes one 23 x 18-cm (9 x 7-in) loaf

4 large eggs

2 egg yolks

$^3/_4$ cup sugar

1 tsp vanilla extract

$1^1/_4$ cups cake flour

$^1/_4$ tsp salt

$^1/_4$ cup warm milk

$^1/_4$ cup butter, melted

Glaze

$^1/_4$ cup butter, melted

$1^1/_2$ Tbsp sugar

- Preheat oven to 160°C (325°F). Grease the base of a 23 x 18-cm (9 x 7-in) loaf pan with butter and dust with flour. Set aside.

- Using an electric mixer fitted with a whisk, whisk eggs and egg yolks on high speed. Add sugar 1 Tbsp at a time. Whisk until pale yellow and fluffy. Add vanilla extract.

- In a separate bowl, whisk together flour and salt and sift.

- Reduce speed to low. Add half the flour and fold into egg mixture. Add milk.

- Fold remaining half of flour into mixture. Whisk in butter.

- Pour batter into prepared loaf pan. Bake for 35 minutes or until a cake tester inserted into the centre of cake comes out clean.

- Remove cake from oven. Brush with melted butter and sprinkle with sugar. Leave to cool completely.

- Store refrigerated. Consume within 4 days.

....

Try This Replace vanilla extract with pandan extract.
For a distinct flavour and colour, add ube (taro flavour) extract.

....

....

Gift Guide Leave in the same pan you baked it in. Cover with pretty paper and tie with a ribbon.

....

This is a rich version of a chiffon cake, said to have been invented by the Chinese. Taisan is light, fluffy and very buttery. It is impossible to stop at just a single slice.

Dark Fruit Cake

Makes one 23-cm (9-in) cake

2 cups glazed fruit

2 cups raisins

1 cup dates

1 cup brandy + $^1/_3$ cup more for brushing

$^1/_4$ cup grape juice

1 cup butter, melted

$^2/_3$ cup dark brown sugar

4 large eggs

1 tsp vanilla extract

1 tsp almond extract

$^1/_2$ tsp orange extract

$1^1/_2$ cups plain (all-purpose) flour

1 tsp baking powder

$^1/_4$ tsp baking soda

$^1/_2$ tsp salt

2 tsp ground cinnamon

1 tsp ground nutmeg

$^1/_4$ tsp ground mace

1 cup walnuts, chopped

- In a mixing bowl, combine glazed fruit, raisins and dates. Add brandy and grape juice. Leave fruit to soak overnight.

- On the day of baking, preheat oven to 180°C (350°F). Line and grease a 23-cm (9-in) square baking pan.

- Using an electric mixer, mix butter and sugar. Add eggs one at a time until completely blended. Mix in vanilla, almond and orange extracts.

- In a separate bowl, whisk together flour, baking powder, baking soda, salt, cinnamon, nutmeg and mace.

- Gradually add flour mixture to butter mixture and mix just until well combined. Fold in fruit mixture and walnuts.

- Pour batter into prepared pan. Bake for 40 to 45 minutes or until a cake tester inserted into the centre of cake comes out clean.

- Brush cake with brandy as soon as it comes out of the oven. Allow to cool completely. Let it sit for a few days before eating.

- Store in the freezer. Consume within a year.

....

Try This Top fruit cake with glazed cherries, assorted nuts and candied orange peel.

....

....

Gift Guide Bake in holiday-themed baking pans for interesting shapes.

....

Be it in Italy where they have the panettone
or in Germany where they have the stollen,
no Christmas is complete without the fruit cake.

Rum Raisin Bundt Cake

Makes one 25-cm (10-in) bundt cake

1 cup raisins

$^1/_4$ cup + $^1/_2$ cup rum

3 cups cake flour

1 Tbsp baking powder

$^1/_2$ tsp salt

$1^1/_2$ cups butter, cut into cubes
    and softened

$1^2/_3$ cups sugar

5 large eggs

1 tsp vanilla extract

$^1/_4$ cup milk

Rum Syrup

$^1/_2$ cup water

$^1/_2$ cup sugar

$^1/_2$ cup dark rum

Sugar Glaze

$^1/_4$ cup icing (confectioner's) sugar

2–3 Tbsp milk

- Soak raisins in $^1/_4$ cup rum. Cover with plastic wrap and refrigerate overnight.

- On day of baking, preheat oven to 180°C (350°F). Grease and flour a 25-cm (10-in) bundt pan. Set aside.

- In a mixing bowl, whisk together flour, baking powder and salt.

- Using an electric mixer, cream butter and sugar on medium speed until light and fluffy. Add eggs one at a time, beating well after each addition. Add vanilla extract.

- Reduce speed to low and alternately add in flour mixture and milk. Add $^1/_2$ cup rum and continue mixing until blended.

- Pour batter into prepared pan. Bake for 55 to 60 minutes or until a cake tester inserted into the centre of cake comes out clean.

- Leave cake in pan. Place on a wire rack to cool for about 20 minutes. Pierce cake several times using a skewer.

- Prepare rum syrup. Combine water and sugar in a small saucepan and simmer for 5 to 10 minutes. Remove from heat, then stir in dark rum. Pour half the rum syrup evenly over cake. Let stand for 30 minutes.

- Prepare sugar glaze. Whisk milk into icing sugar until glaze reaches the right consistency.

- Remove cake from pan and leave to cool completely on a wire rack. Brush cake with remaining syrup and drizzle with sugar glaze before serving. Decorate with dragées.

- Store refrigerated. Consume within a week.

Like fruit cake, this cake improves in flavour with time.

Caramelised Apple Pie

Makes one 23-cm (9-in) pie

10 Granny Smith apples, peeled, cored
    and cut into 2.5-cm (1-in) cubes

1 Tbsp lemon juice

$^2/_3$ cup sugar

$^1/_3$ cup butter

Flaky Pie Dough

$2^1/_2$ cups plain (all-purpose) flour

1 tsp salt

$^3/_4$ cup butter, cut into cubes, chilled

$^1/_4$ cup shortening

$^1/_4$–$^1/_2$ cup iced water

- Prepare pie dough. In a large bowl, mix together flour and salt. Add butter and shortening. Using a fork or pastry cutter, toss flour to coat, then cut in butter and shortening until mixture forms large coarse crumbs, the size of large peas.

- Drizzle with a little iced water and continue tossing until dough is evenly moist and comes together in a mass but does not form into a ball.

- Transfer dough to a floured work surface. Divide dough in half and form each portion into a 15-cm (6-in) disc. Wrap discs in plastic wrap and refrigerate for at least an hour.

- Preheat oven to 190°C (375°F). Prepare a 23-cm (9-in) pie pan.

- Combine apples, lemon juice and sugar in a bowl. Let it stand until apples release their juice, about 10 minutes. Drain, reserving liquid.

- In a heavy frying pan, combine reserved juices and butter. Cook over medium-high heat, stirring frequently, until sugar just begins to caramelise, about 10 minutes. Remove from heat and set aside.

- Roll out a disc of pie dough into a 26-cm (10-in) circle and lay it over pie pan. Trim edges of dough around pan, then crimp the sides using your knuckle or a fork. Place apples in pan, then pour sauce in.

- Roll other disc of dough into a 0.5-cm ($^1/_4$-in) thick sheet. Cut shapes using a leaf cutter to cover the top of pie. Using the back of a knife, draw lines on the leaf to decorate. Lay dough leaves over apple filling and bake for 45 minutes or until crust is golden.

- Leave to cool for 10 minutes before serving. Store refrigerated. Consume within 4 days.

....

Try This Make small tarts instead of a regular pie. Create patterns and designs for the top layer, from the typical lattice design to holiday-themed ones such as hollies and stars.

....

....

Gift Guide Wrap in the same pan you baked it in. Cover with cellophane and tie with a bow on the ends. Bundle it with a pie knife.

....

A flaky melt-in-your-mouth crust matched with
baked caramelised apples—a combination made in dessert heaven.
Top with ice cream for a warm and cold self-indulgent treat.

White Toblerone Cheesecake

Makes one 20-cm (8-in) cake

1^1/$_4$ cups graham cracker crumbs

^{1}/$_4$ cup sugar

^{1}/$_4$ cup butter, melted

Filling

2 cups cream cheese, softened

^{2}/$_3$ cup sugar

4 eggs

2 tsp vanilla extract

100 g (3^1/$_2$ oz) white Toblerone,
  roughly chopped in chunks

Garnish

^{2}/$_3$ cup white chocolate shavings

icing (confectioner's) sugar

^{1}/$_2$ cup strawberries, hulled and halved

- Preheat oven to 120°C (250°F). Using aluminium foil, wrap one side of a 20-cm (8-in) diameter ring mould to create a base. Set aside.

- Prepare crust. In a bowl, combine graham cracker crumbs, sugar and melted butter. Mix well. Spoon mixture into prepared ring mould and press evenly into base. Set aside.

- Prepare filling. Using an electric mixer, beat cream cheese on medium speed. Gradually mix in sugar until well-blended. Add eggs one at a time, mixing well after each addition. Add vanilla.

- Fill mould with half the batter. Add white Toblerone chunks, distributing it evenly. Pour over the remaining batter.

- Bake for 30 to 45 minutes. Turn heat off and leave cake to cool inside oven with door ajar.

- To decorate, sprinkle shaved white chocolate over top of cake. Dust with icing sugar, then decorate with strawberry halves.

- Store refrigerated. Consume within 4 days.

....

Try This Use fresh raspberries instead of strawberries. Graham cracker crumbs can be substituted with crushed shortbread, butter cookies or digestive biscuits.

....

Gift Guide Present in a beautiful charger plate in Christmas colours for an elegant gift.

....

*This cheesecake is rich, creamy and sweet.
The addition of white chocolate curls and
fresh strawberry halves give it that holiday feel.*

Concord Cake

Makes one 20-cm (8-in) cake

Meringue

Egg whites from 5 large eggs

$^3/_4$ cup icing (confectioner's) sugar

1 tsp vanilla extract

$^1/_3$ cup cocoa powder + more for dusting

1 cup icing (confectioner's) sugar

Chocolate Mousse

$1^1/_2$ cups bittersweet chocolate, finely chopped

Egg yolks from 5 large eggs

$1^1/_2$ tsp gelatin powder, dissolved in 3 Tbsp warm water

Egg whites from 5 large eggs

$1^1/_2$ cups double (heavy) cream

- Preheat oven to 120°C (250°F). Draw two 20-cm (8-in) diameter circles on a sheet of parchment paper, 5-cm (2-in) apart. Place on a baking tray. Line another baking tray with parchment paper.

- Prepare meringue. Using an electric mixer, beat egg whites on high speed until soft peaks form. Gradually add sugar and beat to stiff peaks, making it glossy and smooth. Add vanilla. In a separate bowl, sift cocoa powder and icing sugar together. Reduce speed to low and gradually fold icing sugar and cocoa powder mixture into meringue. Mix until just combined.

- Fit a piping bag with a large round tip and fill with meringue. Pipe meringue to fill each 20-cm (8-in) circle in a spiral motion starting from the centre and working outwards. On the other baking tray, pipe long strips of meringue, spacing them 2.5-cm (1-in) apart. Dust meringue strips with cocoa powder.

- Bake for at least $2^1/_2$ hours or until meringue is crisp and thoroughly dry. Leave to cool completely before peeling off paper carefully. Store in an airtight container.

- Prepare chocolate mousse. In a double boiler, melt chocolate until smooth. Whisk in egg yolks, then add gelatin and mix well. Transfer mixture to a bigger bowl. Using an electric mixer, whip egg whites to stiff peaks. Gently fold whipped whites into chocolate mixture in 2 additions. In another bowl, whip cream to firm peaks. Fold into chocolate mixture.

- To assemble cake, place a meringue disc in the bottom of a 20-cm (8-in) ring mould lined with acetate on the side. Pour half the mousse over the meringue disc. Place second disc over and pour rest of mousse over disc. Use a metal spatula to level off mousse. Place in the freezer for 2 to 3 hours or until completely set.

- To decorate, remove cake from mould. Leave at room temperature for about 10 minutes to defrost a little. Cut meringue strips into 5-cm (2-in) lengths and use to decorate top and sides of cake. Dust with cocoa powder before serving.

- Store refrigerated. Consume within 4 days.

....

Try This Turn this into miniature cakes.

....

....

Gift Guide Place on a cake stand with a glass dish cover. Or tie a loose bow around the cake.

*It's chocolate through and through and plays on textures
with its crunchy base and smooth mousse. It's perfect as it is.*

Bagged

Candied Nuts

Makes 4 cups

4 Tbsp butter

$^2/_3$ cup caster sugar

$^1/_4$ tsp salt

1 Tbsp cream

$^1/_2$ tsp ground cinnamon

$^1/_2$ tsp cayenne pepper

1 cup cashew nuts

1 cup almonds

1 cup pecans

1 cup peanuts

- Line a baking pan with parchment paper or a silicon mat. Set aside.
- In a large saucepan over medium heat, mix butter, sugar and salt.
- When sugar is completely dissolved, add cream, cinnamon and cayenne pepper. Stir well.
- Stir in nuts. Cook until mixture is slightly thick and coats nuts. Be careful not to burn it.
- Transfer to prepared baking pan and allow to cool and harden before breaking into pieces.
- Store in an airtight container. Keep in a cool, dry place. Consume within a week.

....

Try This Vary the nuts as desired, such as making it all pecan or a mix of your favourites.

....

....

Gift Guide Use colourful plastic containers your loved ones can keep and reuse.

....

You can make it subtly spicy or just plain sweet.
Whatever your preference, these will surely be tastier than regular nuts.

Flavoured Butters

Makes $1/2$ cup of each flavour

Herbed Bacon Butter

$1/2$ cup unsalted butter, softened

1 tsp dried oregano

5 strips bacon, fried until crisp, then crumbled

Maple-Cinnamon Butter

$1/2$ cup unsalted butter, softened

6 Tbsp maple syrup

1 tsp ground cinnamon

- For either butter, simply mix everything until well-combined.
- Place on a sheet of plastic wrap. Roll and shape into a log.
- Refrigerate until firm, about 30 minutes.
- Slice and use as needed.
- Store refrigerated. Use within 3 months.

Try This Use any leftover herbs from your refrigerator.

Gift Guide Tie each end of the log with a ribbon and label. Make sure it's frozen when you give it to your loved one.

Versatile in flavour and use, these butters can be enjoyed simply spread on toast.

Chocolate-dipped Pretzels

Makes 24 pretzels

24 whole pretzels
$1^1/_2$ cups dark coating chocolate, melted
Sprinkles

- Line 2 to 3 baking trays with parchment paper or silicon mats.
- Using a fork, dip pretzels one at a time into melted chocolate, making sure that pretzels are well-coated.
- Lay coated pretzels on prepared trays. Leave to set slightly, then decorate with sprinkles. Leave to set completely.
- Store in plastic bags or airtight containers. Keep in a cool, dry place. Consume within 2 weeks.

....

Try This Other coloured coating chocolates can be used as desired.

....
....

Gift Guide Place different-coloured pretzels in a box.
You can also include other chocolate-dipped items such as dried fruit and nuts.

....

This German classic is given a makeover with a chocolate coating. They're perfect to keep in the bag for that sudden sweet craving.

Holiday Snowballs

Makes about 30 cookies

1 cup butter, cut into cubes and softened

$^3/_4$ cup icing (confectioner's) sugar +
   1 cup for coating

$2^1/_3$ cups plain (all-purpose) flour

1 cup hazelnuts, toasted and chopped

- Preheat oven to 190°C (375°F). Line 2 to 3 baking trays with parchment paper or silicon mats.

- Using an electric mixer, beat butter and $^3/_4$ cup icing sugar on medium speed until light and fluffy.

- Reduce speed to low. Add flour and nuts. Beat until just combined.

- Using a small 20-g ($^2/_3$-oz) ice cream scoop, portion out dough and roll into balls.

- Place balls onto prepared trays, spacing them 5 cm (2 in) apart.

- Bake for 12 to 15 minutes or until lightly golden in colour.

- Allow cookies to cool for 5 minutes before rolling in icing sugar to coat. Place on a wire rack to cool completely.

- Store in an airtight container. Keep in a cool, dry place. Consume within 4 days.

....

Try This Sift the icing sugar with some ground cinnamon before using to coat the cookies. Vary the nuts as desired.

....

....

Gift Guide Pair these cookies with a box of assorted tea.

....

These bite-size cookies are typically served during special occasions such as weddings and Christmas.

French Macarons

Makes about 30 macarons

200 g (7 oz) icing (confectioner's) sugar
  + $^1/_4$ cup for dusting

150 g (5 oz) ground almond

Egg whites from 3 large eggs

2 Tbsp sugar

Filling

$^1/_4$ cup cherry jam

$^1/_2$ Tbsp cherry gelatin powder

$1^1/_2$ cups white chocolate, melted

- Line 2 to 3 baking trays with parchment paper or silicon mats. Create a template for piping macarons. Cut paper to fit baking tray, then trace circles about 2.5-cm (1-in) in diameter on paper, keeping them about 4 cm ($1^1/_2$ in) apart. Set aside.

- Combine icing sugar and ground almond. Mix well and sift twice.

- Using an electric mixer, whisk egg whites to soft peaks. Add sugar 1 Tbsp at a time. Beat to stiff peaks.

- Fold icing sugar and ground almond mixture gently into egg whites until mixture is glossy and well combined.

- Spoon mixture into a piping bag fitted with 0.5-cm ($^1/_4$-in) round tip. Place template under parchment paper or silicon mat and pipe on prepared baking trays, spacing macarons 5-cm (2-in) apart.

- Allow piped macarons to rest at room temperature for about an hour or until mixture doesn't stick to your finger when touched. The timing is dependent on the humidity of the room. When macarons are ready, preheat a fan-assisted oven to 150°C (300°F).

- Bake for 12 to 14 minutes or until firm to touch. Remove from oven and set aside to cool completely.

- Prepare filling. Place cherry jam and gelatin powder in a small saucepan. Heat until jam is melted and gelatin is dissolved. Remove from heat and allow to cool for 5 minutes.

- Gradually add cherry mixture to melted white chocolate. Whisk vigorously to prevent mixture from getting lumpy. Whisk until mixture is smooth and glossy. Spoon filling into a piping bag fitted with a 0.5-cm ($^1/_4$-in) diameter round tip.

- Pipe a teaspoon of filling over the flat side of a macaron, then sandwich with another macaron. Place on a baking tray. Dust lightly with icing sugar before serving.

- Store in an airtight container. Keep refrigerated. Consume within 4 days.

Tip: If your oven is not fan-assisted, you need to set it at a slightly higher temperature, about 5°C to 10°C (10°F to 20°F). French macarons are very sensitive to heat so it is best to test bake a few pieces on a tray to find the ideal temperature.

Try This Mix and match flavours. Macarons can be made in a wide range of flavours, from traditional flavours like vanilla and chocolate to contemporary flavours like rose or matcha. The same goes for the fillings. Use jams, ganache or buttercream.

Gift Guide Build a beautiful macaron tower and let it be the centrepiece and topic of conversation at your party.

Delicate, light and chewy, these beautiful meringue pillows are so addictive, you might end up keeping them all to yourself!

Olive Palmiers

Makes 18 cookies

1 sheet puff pastry, 25-cm (10-in) square

$^1/_3$ cup olive tapenade (page 40), drained

- Preheat oven to 200°C (400°F). Line 2 baking trays with parchment paper or silicon mats.

- Lay puff pastry on a working surface. Spread with olive tapenade.

- Roll 2 opposite ends of puff pastry towards the centre to meet.

- Cut roll into 0.5-cm ($^1/_4$-in) slices. Shape slices into a V-shape with the two sides curving out slightly. Place palmiers on prepared trays.

- Bake for 15 to 20 minutes or until palmiers are puffed and golden. Serve warm or at room temperature.

- Store in an airtight container. Keep in a cool, dry place. Consume within 4 days.

....

Try This As a sweet alternative, replace tapenade with cinnamon-sugar.

....
....

Gift Guide Pile palmiers in a decorative bowl or a wide-rimmed glass vase.

....

Named after palm trees, palmiers can be made sweet or savoury. Whatever you fancy, satisfaction will definitely be guaranteed.

Shortbread Stars

Makes about 48 cookies

1 cup butter, cut into cubes and softened
$^1/_2$ cup sugar
1 tsp vanilla extract
$1^1/_2$ cups plain (all-purpose) flour
$^1/_3$ cup rice flour
1 cup icing (confectioner's) sugar

- Line baking trays with greased parchment paper or silicon mats. Set aside.
- Using an electric mixer, beat butter and sugar until light and fluffy. Add vanilla extract. Mix well.
- Gradually add flours and mix to form a dough.
- Cover dough with plastic wrap and chill for at least 30 minutes.
- Preheat oven to 160°C (325°F).
- Roll chilled dough between 2 sheets of plastic wrap or parchment paper to 0.3-cm ($^1/_8$-in) thick.
- Cut out dough using star-shaped cookie cutters. Place on prepared baking trays.
- Bake for 15 to 20 minutes or until slightly golden around the edges. Dust with icing sugar.
- Remove from tray and leave to cool completely on a wire rack.
- Store in an airtight container. Keep in a cool, dry place. Consume within 4 days.

....

Try This Use cookie cutters of holiday shapes.

....

....

Gift Guide Place assorted shapes in a tea cup or sake cup.
Wrap with a clear cellophane and tie with ribbon.

....

These are traditional Christmas cookies.
This recipe uses rice flour as well
which makes the cookies flakier and lighter.

Peppermint Meringue

Makes 120 pieces

1 cup egg whites

1 cup sugar

$1^3/_4$ cups icing (confectioner's) sugar

2 drops peppermint oil

Red and green icing gel

- Preheat oven to 95°C (200°F). Line baking trays with greased parchment paper or silicon mats.

- Using an electric mixer, beat egg whites to soft peaks. Gradually add sugar 1 Tbsp at a time. Beat until stiff.

- Reduce speed to low and gradually add icing sugar. Mix until well combined. Add peppermint oil. Stir well.

- Prepare a piping bag and fit it with a star tip (no. 826). Using a paintbrush, brush the inside of the bag with 2 red and 2 green alternate stripes down the length. Space them out evenly.

- Spoon the meringue into the piping bag, then pipe meringue on prepared baking trays, each about 5 cm (2 in) in diameter.

- Bake for $1^1/_2$ to 2 hours. Turn off heat and leave meringue to cool completely inside the oven.

- Store in an airtight container. Keep in a cool, dry place. Consume within 4 days.

....

Try This Use icing gel of different colours to match your holiday theme.

....

....

Gift Guide Build a miniature Christmas tree using meringues.
Pile them high and keep them steady using melted chocolate.

....

Warning:
These delicate little sweets
can be very addictive!
Enjoy as is or stack
in a glass alternately with
softly whipped cream and
sliced fresh fruit
for a festive dessert.

Almond Butter Crunch

Makes a 30 x 23-cm (12 x 9-in) pan

1 cup butter

1 cup sugar

$^1/_4$ cup water

$^1/_4$ tsp salt

1 tsp vanilla extract

1 tsp baking soda

2 cups, dark coating chocolate, melted

$1^1/_4$ cups almonds, toasted and chopped

- Lightly grease a 30 x 23-cm (12 x 9-in) baking pan. Set aside.

- In a medium saucepan, stir together butter, sugar, water, salt and vanilla extract. Bring to the boil, stirring constantly. Cook until temperature reaches 155°C (310°F) on a candy thermometer and mixture is light caramel in colour.

- Add baking soda and stir. Be careful as it will foam up.

- Pour mixture into prepared baking pan and leave to cool completely to room temperature. Wipe off excess butter on surface with a tissue.

- Using a double boiler, melt half the quantity of chocolate and stir until smooth. Spread evenly over butter crunch layer and top with half the almonds before chocolate starts to set. Allow to fully set.

- Melt remaining chocolate.

- Unmould butter crunch layer keeping chocolate and nut layer on the underside. Spread with melted chocolate, then sprinkle with remainder of almonds. Allow to fully set.

- Break butter crunch into large pieces. Store in an airtight container or seal in plastic.

- Keep in a cool, dry place away from moisture. Consume within a week.

....

Try This Use white chocolate in place of dark chocolate.

....

....

Gift Guide Leave butter crunch whole or in big shards
and provide a small hammer or cleaver for cutting to the desired size.

....

*Toffee candy sandwiched in
a layer of chocolate
and chopped nuts.
Pure indulgence!
It's crunch time!*

Chocolate Peppermint Bark

Makes a 30 x 23 (12 x 9-in) sheet

$1^1/_2$ cups white coating chocolate, melted

$1^1/_2$ cups dark coating chocolate

1 cup peppermint candies, slightly crushed

- Line the base of a 30 x 23 (12 x 9-in) pan with parchment paper or a silicon mat.

- Pour melted white chocolate into pan and spread evenly using an offset spatula. Leave to set completely at room temperature.

- When white chocolate has set, melt dark chocolate and pour over white chocolate layer. Spread evenly. Sprinkle peppermint candies uniformly over surface.

- Allow dark chocolate to set completely at room temperature. Takes about 1 hour.

- Break chocolate into pieces. Pack into plastic bags or store in airtight containers. Keep in a cool, dry place. Consume within a week.

....

Try This Swirl the white and dark chocolate together. Sprinkle with granola.

....

....

Gift Guide Place in pretty plastic pots.

....

A sweet sheet made with two kinds of chocolate is made even more playful with the sprinkling of crushed peppermint candies.

Snowflake Marshmallows

Makes 2 trays, each 30 x 23-in (12 x 9-in)

2 Tbsp gelatin powder

$1/2$ cup warm water

$1^1/2$ cups sugar

$3/4$ cup glucose

$1/3$ cup water

$1/4$ tsp vanilla extract

1 cup icing (confectioner's) sugar

$1/4$ cup corn flour (cornstarch)

- Line two 30 x 23-in (12 x 9-in) baking trays with parchment paper and grease lightly.

- In the bowl of an electric mixer, place gelatin and warm water. Stir well until gelatin is completely dissolved.

- In a saucepan, combine sugar, glucose and water. Stir until sugar is dissolved. Bring mixture to the boil. Do not stir anymore from this stage. Cook until temperature reaches 115°C (240°F) on a candy thermometer. Remove from heat.

- Whisk gelatin and water mixture on high speed. Gradually pour hot sugar syrup into gelatin mixture.

- Add vanilla extract. Whisk until mixture is thick and fluffy.

- Pour mixture equally into prepared trays. Cover top with plastic wrap and leave to set overnight in the refrigerator.

- The next day, combine icing sugar and corn flour in a small bowl. Mix well.

- Dust a work surface with some corn flour mixture. Turn over marshmallow on the work surface. Dip a snowflake cutter in corn flour mixture and cut through marshmallow.

- Dust marshmallow snowflakes with additional corn flour mixture.

- Store in an airtight container. Keep in a cool, dry place. Consume within a week.

Try This Add colour to your marshmallows by mixing food colouring with the sugar syrup.

Gift Guide Pack with a bag of hot chocolate and mugs in a box.

Home-made and yes, yummy too.
It's not difficult to do and making your own
means that you can cut them into holiday shapes.

Caramel Popcorn

Makes 3 cups

$1/2$ cup brown sugar

4 Tbsp butter, melted

2 Tbsp light corn syrup

$1/4$ tsp salt

$1/4$ tsp baking soda

3 cups plain popcorn

- Line a baking pan with parchment paper or a silicon mat. Set aside.
- In a medium saucepan, combine sugar, butter, corn syrup and salt. Stir until sugar is just dissolved.
- Cook over low to medium heat until amber in colour. Remove from heat.
- Stir in baking soda. Be careful as the mixture will foam up.
- Once well mixed, pour mixture over popcorn in a bowl and mix using a wooden spoon.
- Pour onto prepared baking pan, separating popcorn so they don't form large clusters. Leave to cool.
- Store in airtight containers. Keep in a cool, dry place. Consume within a week.

....

Try This Add a dash of cayenne pepper to make it slightly spicy or mix in some nuts for added texture.

....
....

Gift Guide Place in classic popcorn containers and bag it. Or how about tin pails? Cute.

....

*This party-perfect crunchy treat
will have you popping one after another.*

Orange, Cranberry & Pistachio Biscotti

Makes about 20 biscotti

$2^3/_4$ cups plain (all-purpose) flour

2 tsp baking powder

$1/_2$ tsp salt

$1/_3$ cup butter, cut into cubes and softened

$3/_4$ cup sugar

2 large eggs

1 tsp orange extract

1 Tbsp orange zest

1 cup dried cranberries

1 cup pistachio nuts

- Preheat oven to 160°C (325°F).

- In a bowl, whisk together flour, baking powder and salt.

- Using an electric mixer, beat butter and sugar until light and fluffy. Mix in eggs, orange extract and orange zest. Reduce speed to low and gradually add flour mixture to butter mixture until incorporated. Fold in cranberries and pistachios.

- Transfer dough to a lightly floured work surface. Knead until smooth and not too sticky. Shape dough into a log, 10-cm (4-in) wide and 2.5-cm (1-in) thick. Place on a baking tray.

- Bake for 35 to 40 minutes or until loaf is golden around the edges.

- Allow to cool slightly, then slice into 1-cm ($1/_2$-in) thick slices using a large, sharp knife. Place flat on a baking tray.

- Lower oven temperature to 150°C (300°F) and return cookies to the oven to bake for another 20 to 25 minutes. Transfer to a wire rack to cool.

- Store in an airtight container. Keep in a cool, dry place. Consume within a week.

....

Try This Make it extra indulgent by dipping the biscotti in chocolate.

....

....

Gift Guide Place biscotti neatly inside a plastic bag or a tall mug.

....

These twice-baked Italian cookies
are typically served with a drink
which they can be dunked into and enjoyed.

Chocolate Chip Espresso Cookies

Makes 12 large cookies

1 cup butter, cut into cubes and softened

$^2/_3$ cup sugar

1$^1/_4$ cups dark brown sugar

2 large eggs

1 tsp vanilla extract

2$^2/_3$ cups plain (all-purpose) flour

1 tsp baking soda

1 tsp salt

3 Tbsp coarsely ground espresso beans

3 cups semi-sweet chocolate chips

- Using an electric mixer, beat together butter and sugars until light and fluffy. Mix in eggs one at a time until completely blended. Mix in vanilla extract.

- In a separate bowl, whisk together flour, baking soda and salt.

- Reduce speed to low and gradually add flour mixture to butter mixture and mix until incorporated. Fold in ground espresso and semi-sweet chocolate chips.

- Place dough in an airtight container and refrigerate for at least 1 hour or overnight before baking.

- Remove dough from refrigerator and thaw at room temperature for 15 to 20 minutes.

- Preheat oven to 190°C (375°F). Line 2 to 3 baking trays with parchment paper or silicon mats.

- Using a 110-g (4-oz) ice cream scoop, spoon dough onto prepared baking trays, spacing them about 5 cm (2 in) apart.

- Bake for 9 to 12 minutes or until edges of cookies are slightly golden and centre is still slightly soft. Allow to cool for about 5 minutes before serving.

- Store in an airtight container. Keep in a cool, dry place. Consume within 4 days.

Try This Use different chocolate chips.

Gift Guide Insert giant cookies into CD sleeves, stack in threes and tie with a bow.

This sweet treat is for the ultimate coffee lover.
The addition of coffee enhances the flavour of chocolate and vice versa.

Death by Chocolate Cookies

Makes 10 cookies

$1^1/_3$ cups bittersweet chocolate, melted

$^3/_4$ cup dark brown sugar

$^1/_4$ cup butter, melted

2 large eggs

1 tsp vanilla extract

$^2/_3$ cup plain (all-purpose) flour

$^1/_4$ tsp baking powder

$^1/_8$ tsp salt

$^2/_3$ cup white chocolate, cut into cubes

$^2/_3$ cup milk chocolate, cut into cubes

1 cup macadamia nuts

- In a mixing bowl, combine melted chocolate, sugar and butter. Mix until well combined. Add eggs one at a time and mix until completely blended. Mix in vanilla extract.

- In a separate bowl, whisk together flour, baking powder and salt.

- Gradually add flour mixture to chocolate mixture and mix just until well combined. Fold in white and milk chocolate and macadamia nuts.

- Place dough in an airtight container and refrigerate for at least 1 hour or overnight before baking. When ready to bake, remove dough from the refrigerator and thaw at room temperature for 10 to 15 minutes.

- Preheat oven to 180°C (350°F). Line baking trays with parchment paper or silicon mats.

- Using a 55-g (2-oz) ice cream scoop, scoop dough onto prepared baking trays, spacing them about 5 cm (2 in) apart.

- Bake for 8 to 10 minutes or until edges are set and centre is still slightly soft.

- Allow to cool for about 5 minutes before serving. Leave to cool completely before storing in an airtight container. Keep in a cool, dry place. Consume within 4 days.

Try This Vary this recipe by using different nuts.

Gift Guide Stack several cookies together and tie with a ribbon. Place in unconventional containers or simply in a glass cookie jar.

A chocoholic's dream.
It's chunky, chewy and nutty,
making it simply hard to resist.

Gingerbread Cookies

Makes 25 to 30 cookies

$^1/_2$ cup butter, cut into cubes, softened

$^1/_3$ cup sugar

1 large egg

$^1/_4$ cup honey

$^1/_4$ cup molasses

$2^3/_4$ cups plain (all-purpose) flour

$^1/_2$ tsp baking soda

$^1/_2$ tsp salt

$^1/_2$ Tbsp ground ginger

$^1/_2$ Tbsp ground cinnamon

$^1/_2$ tsp ground cloves

$^1/_2$ tsp ground nutmeg

Icing

4 cups icing (confectioner's) sugar

Egg whites from 2 eggs

- Using an electric mixer, beat butter and sugar at medium-high speed until light and fluffy. Reduce speed to low. Add egg and beat well. Add honey and molasses. Mix well.

- In a separate bowl, whisk together flour, baking soda, salt and spices. Gradually add flour mixture to butter mixture and beat until just combined.

- Divide dough into 3 equal portions and wrap each in plastic. Refrigerate for 1 hour. Remove dough from refrigerator and let stand at room temperature for about 10 minutes.

- Line a work surface with parchment paper. Dust lightly with flour, then roll out dough on parchment paper to 0.5-cm ($^1/_4$-in) thick. Dust and flour as necessary to prevent dough from sticking. Alternatively, roll dough between 2 sheets of parchment paper.

- Leaving dough on parchment paper, transfer to baking trays and place in the freezer for about 15 minutes.

- Preheat oven to 160°C (325°F). Line baking trays with parchment paper or silicon mats.

- Remove dough from freezer and immediately cut using cookie cutters. Place on prepared baking trays and bake for 15 to 20 minutes or until edges are slightly golden, rotating trays halfway through. Leave to cool on wire racks before decorating.

- Prepare icing. Using an electric mixer, beat icing sugar and egg whites on low speed for 5 to 8 minutes to mix. Spoon into a piping bag fitted with a small round tip (no. 4) and decorate. Allow icing to set.

- Store in airtight containers. Consume within a week.

Try This Colour the icing by dipping the tip of a toothpick into some food colouring and gradually mixing it into the icing until the desired colour is achieved. Make a gingerbread house and decorate with a variety of candies.

Gift Guide Wrap in transparent plastic, tie with ribbon and hang on the Christmas tree.

This is another staple come holidays.
And the wonderful thing about it is that it
allows you to create wonderful shapes and colours
both kids and kids-at-heart will like.

Holiday Sugar Cookies

Makes 40 to 50 cookies

$^1/_2$ cup butter, cut into cubes and softened

1 cup sugar

1 large egg

1 tsp almond extract

2 cups plain (all-purpose) flour

$^1/_2$ tsp baking powder

$^1/_4$ tsp salt

Icing

4 cups icing (confectioner's) sugar

Egg whites from 2 large eggs

Food colouring

- Using an electric mixer, beat butter and sugar on medium speed until light and fluffy. Mix in egg and almond extract.

- In a separate bowl, sift together flour, baking powder and salt.

- Reduce speed to low. Gradually add flour mixture to butter mixture until dough forms.

- Flatten dough into a disc and cover with plastic wrap. Refrigerate for 1 hour before rolling and cutting.

- Preheat oven to 160°C (325°F). Line baking trays with parchment paper or silicon mats. Set aside.

- Line a work surface with parchment paper. Dust lightly with flour, then roll out dough on parchment paper to 0.5-cm ($^1/_4$-in) thick. Dust and flour as necessary to prevent dough from sticking. Alternatively, roll dough between 2 sheets of parchment paper.

- Leaving dough on parchment paper, transfer to baking trays and place in the freezer for about 15 minutes.

- Preheat oven to 160°C (325°F). Line several baking trays with parchment paper.

- Remove dough from freezer and immediately cut using cookie cutters. Place on prepared baking trays and bake for 15 to 20 minutes or until edges are slightly golden, rotating trays halfway through. Leave to cool on wire racks before decorating.

- Prepare icing. Using an electric mixer, beat icing sugar and egg whites on low speed for 5 to 8 minutes to mix. Set aside a portion of the white icing for decoration. Dip the tip of a toothpick in food colouring and gradually mix into the icing until desired colour is achieved.

- To decorate, dip one side of a cookie in icing. Scrape off excess and smoothen. Leave icing (coating) to set completely before decorating. Using the white icing, make a zigzag pattern across the cookie and stick silver dragées on the ends. Allow to dry completely before storing.

- Store in an airtight container. Keep in a cool, dry place. Consume within 4 days.

Caught in the mad Christmas rush? No worries.
You can make the dough days ahead and leave it in the freezer.

Parmesan Sticks

Makes 12 sticks

1 sheet puff pastry, 25-cm (10-in) square
1–2 Tbsp butter, melted
$^1/_2$ tsp coarsely cracked black pepper
$^1/_4$ cup grated Parmesan cheese

- Preheat oven to 200°C (400°F). Line 2 baking trays with parchment paper or silicon mats. Set aside.
- Lay sheet of puff pastry on a work surface and brush with melted butter. Sprinkle over freshly cracked pepper and grated cheese.
- Using a fluted pastry wheel, cut sheet into 12 strips, each approximately 2-cm ($^3/_4$-in) wide.
- Twist each strip 3 to 4 times, then place strips on prepared baking trays and bake for 15 to 20 minutes or until strips are puffed and golden.
- Serve warm or at room temperature.
- Store in an airtight container. Keep in a cool, dry place. Consume within 4 days.

Tip: You have to work on the puff pastry quickly so it will be easier to handle. Once it gets soft, return to the freezer and chill for a couple of minutes before continuing.

....

Try This Instead of using cheese, flavour your breadsticks with paprika, or toasted sesame seeds and spices.

....

Gift Guide Place a bundle of breadsticks in a bread basket or carafe and wrap with plastic.

....

Store-bought puff pastry makes baking this a cinch.
Place in the middle of a table and everyone
will soon gather and start munching.

Cinnamon Rolls

Makes 7 rolls

$^1/_2$ Tbsp active dry yeast

$^1/_2$ cup lukewarm water

$^1/_4$ cup sugar

$^1/_2$ cup butter, softened

1 large egg

2 cups bread flour

$^1/_2$ tsp salt

Filling

$^1/_3$ cup butter, softened

$^1/_2$ cup dark brown sugar

$1^1/_2$ Tbsp ground cinnamon

Icing (Optional)

$^1/_3$ cup butter, softened

$^1/_4$ cup cream cheese

$^1/_2$ cup icing (confectioner's) sugar

$^1/_2$ tsp vanilla extract

- In the bowl of an electric mixer, dissolve yeast in lukewarm water. Stir and leave for about 5 minutes until bubbly.

- Using a dough hook, run mixer on low speed. Add sugar, butter and egg. Gradually add flour and salt and knead until mixture forms a smooth elastic dough, about 15 minutes.

- Transfer dough to a greased bowl, cover with a damp towel and leave in a warm place. Allow dough to rise until doubled in size, about 1 hour.

- Punch dough down, then transfer to a floured work surface. Roll dough into a rectangular sheet about 25-cm (10-in) long, 20-cm (8-in) wide and 0.5-cm ($^1/_4$-in) thick.

- Using a spatula, spread softened butter evenly over dough. In a small bowl, combine sugar and cinnamon, then sprinkle buttered surface with cinnamon-sugar.

- Starting from one long side, roll dough, pressing lightly to form a tight log. Roll until you reach the other end. Pinch seam to seal end.

- Cut roll into 7 equal slices. Place into a 23-cm (9-in) greased baking pan. Allow to rise until doubled in size, about 30 to 45 minutes.

- Preheat oven to 190°C (375°F). Bake rolls for 12 to 15 minutes or until golden.

- To make icing, cream butter and cream cheese. Gradually add icing sugar, then vanilla. Spread icing over freshly baked rolls or serve on the side. Store refrigerated. Consume within 3 days

....

Try This For additional texture, add nuts or chocolate chips to the filling.

....

....

Gift Guide Leave rolls in the pan you baked them in. Wrap and tie with a ribbon.

....

As soon as these rolls come out of the oven,
a sweet cinnamon buttery scent surrounds the kitchen,
making it impossible for you to resist them.

Herbed Focaccia

Makes one 25-cm (10-in) diameter loaf

$^3/_4$ cup lukewarm water

1 Tbsp honey

1 tsp active dry yeast

$^1/_4$ cup olive oil

$^1/_2$ Tbsp sea salt + more for sprinkling

$1^3/_4$ cups bread flour

4 Tbsp extra virgin olive oil

1 Tbsp rosemary leaves

1–2 tsp Italian seasoning

- In the bowl of an electric mixer, combine lukewarm water, honey and yeast. Stir until well combined. Leave for about 5 minutes or until bubbly.

- Using a paddle attachment at low speed, add olive oil, then $^1/_2$ Tbsp salt. Add flour in batches. Knead until mixture forms a smooth elastic dough, about 15 minutes.

- Transfer dough to a greased bowl, cover with a damp towel and leave in a warm place. Allow dough to rise until doubled in size, about 45 minutes to 1 hour.

- Grease a 25-cm (10-in) round baking pan with 2 Tbsp extra virgin olive oil. Place dough in pan and leave to rest for 10 to 15 minutes.

- Flip rested dough over so that the oiled surface faces up. Gently stretch dough towards edge of pan. Using your fingertips, dimple dough. Drizzle with remaining extra virgin olive oil. Sprinkle with herbs and $^1/_4$ to $^1/_2$ tsp salt.

- Leave to rise in a warm area until doubled in size, about 45 minutes.

- Preheat oven to 190°C (375°F).

- Place pan in oven and bake focaccia for 12 to 15 minutes or until top is golden and crisp. Remove focaccia to a wire rack and leave to cool completely.

- Store in an airtight container at room temperature for up to 2 days or refrigerate for a longer shelf life.

....

Try This Embed pitted olives in the dough for a lovely dotted focaccia.
Bake in a rectangular pan for something different.

....

....

Gift Guide Cradle in a lovely piece of cloth or place on a chopping board and wrap.

....

Traditionally, Italian children enjoyed this bread
during their school break. But this bread is so good,
it is now enjoyed the world over by both children and adults!

Hot Cocoa Mix

Makes 3^1/$_2$ cups

1 cup cocoa powder

1 cup powdered milk

1^1/$_2$ cups sugar

- Sift cocoa powder, powdered milk and sugar into a mixing bowl. Mix with a wire whisk until completely blended.

- Place in a plastic bag and seal with a sticker. Place in a cool, dry place. Use within a month.

- To use, scoop 2 Tbsp cocoa mix and dissolve in ^{3}/$_4$ cup hot milk. Top with a dollop of whipped cream or marshmallows.

....

Try This Spice up your drink with a bit of cayenne or cinnamon.

....
....

Gift Guide Place all the ingredients in a jar, layering each dry ingredient on top of the other and provide instructions to mix the ingredients and use the cocoa mix.

....

*Cap off holiday nights with a steaming mug of
hot chocolate that can be made in an instant.*

Cooking Notes

Sterilising Jars

Wash the jars and lids in warm soapy water. Place in a pot, cover with water, then boil for 12 minutes. Drain off any liquid, then transfer to a baking tray lined with parchment paper. Use tongs that have been washed and boiled along with the bottles. Allow to dry in a preheated oven at 100°C (210°F). Now the jars are ready for use.

All About Chocolate

The chocolates used in this book are:

- Couverture chocolate used for ganache and truffles, brownies and cookies.
- Compound coating chocolate used for coating and dipping.

Both kinds are available in groceries and most baking supply stores.

Here are a few guidelines on how to care for your chocolates.

Storing Chocolate

Chocolate has a long shelf life. If stored and cared for properly, dark chocolate can last for about 12 months while milk and white chocolate can last for about 6 months. To guarantee the good quality of chocolates, abide by these rules:

- Store at cool room temperature (about 18°C/65°F).
- Place in an airtight container.
- Do not refrigerate or store in the freezer as this will introduce moisture that can affect the appearance and viscosity of chocolate.

Melting Chocolate

There are two ways that you can melt chocolate:

- In a bowl placed over a pot of simmering water. Make sure that the bowl does not touch the surface of the water. Stir occasionally until the chocolate becomes glossy and smooth.
- In a microwave-safe bowl. Place in the microwave oven and heat for 20 to 30 seconds at low to medium heat. Remove the bowl and stir, then return to the microwave oven and heat for another 20 seconds and stir again. Repeat this several times until the chocolate is completely melted and is glossy and smooth.

Note: If you are using chocolate for coating and dipping and the chocolate starts to set, you may repeat the procedure for melting to continue working with the chocolate.

Gift Basket Combos

Here is a list of ideas to help you put together the perfect gift for your loved ones, whatever the gifting occasion!

Meal Starters
Marinated Feta (page 48)
Olive Palmiers (page 118)
Mediterranean Dipping Oil (page 20)
Crostini

Hot Off the Grill
Flavoured Butters (page 110)
BBQ Sauce (page 24)
Trio of Rubs (page 18)
Choice meat

Tea Party
Smoked Salmon Spread (page 42)
Marinated Olives (page 50)
Parmesan Sticks (page 142)
Tea

Spread the Love
Olive Tapenade (page 40)
Cheese Torta (page 88)
Chicken Liver Pâté (page 36)
Butter knife

Condiment Crazy
Chunky Mango-Lemon Chutney (page 46)
Chilli Jam (page 44)
Ketchup (page 26)
Side plates or bowls

Choco Cravings
Death by Chocolate Cookies (page 136)
Chocolate Peppermint Bark (page 126)
Hot Cocoa Mix (page 148)
Chocolate bar

White Christmas
Snowflake Marshmallows (page 128)
Holiday Snowballs (page 114)
Alfajores (page 78)
White chocolate

Orange Bounty
Orange, Cranberry & Pistachio Biscotti (page 132)
Orange-Tarragon Vinaigrette (page 56)
Orange-Berry Vodka (page 64)
Mandarin oranges

Italian Fare
Grilled Vegetable Antipasto (page 58)
Herbed Focaccia (page 146)
Two Pesto Sauces (page 34)
Pasta noodles

The Morning After
Granola (page 60)
Chocolate Chip Espresso Cookies (page 134)
Ensaymada (page 92)
Coffee

On-the-Road
Candied Nuts (page 108)
Chocolate-dipped Pretzels (page 112)
Caramel Popcorn (page 130)
CDs

Fruit Fest
Preserved Lemons (page 62)
Caramelised Apple Pie (page 100)
Apricot Macadamia Brownies (page 72)
Fresh fruit

Weights & Measures

Metric and Imperial Measurement Equivalents

Quantities in this book are given in American spoon and cup measures. The metric and imperial measurement equivalents for these spoon and cup measures are listed here.

Dry Measures

Metric	Imperial
15 g	$^1/_2$ oz
30 g	1 oz
45 g	$1^1/_2$ oz
60 g	2 oz
75 g	$2^1/_2$ oz
90 g	3 oz
105 g	$3^1/_2$ oz
120 g	4 oz
150 g	5 oz
180 g	6 oz
200 g	7 oz
225 g	8 oz
255 g	9 oz
285 g	10 oz
315 g	11 oz
340 g	12 oz
370 g	13 oz
400 g	14 oz
430 g	15 oz
455 g	16 oz

Liquid and Volume Measures

Metric	Imperial	Spoon/Cup
5 ml	$^1/_6$ fl oz	1 tsp
15 ml	$^1/_2$ fl oz	1 Tbsp
30 ml	1 fl oz	2 Tbsp
45 ml	$1^1/_2$ fl oz	3 Tbsp
60 ml	2 fl oz	$^1/_4$ cup
120 ml	4 fl oz	$^1/_2$ cup
180 ml	6 fl oz	$^3/_4$ cup
240 ml	8 fl oz	1 cup
300 ml	10 fl oz	$1^1/_4$ cups
360 ml	12 fl oz	$1^1/_2$ cups
420 ml	14 fl oz	$1^3/_4$ cups
480 ml	16 fl oz	2 cups
540 ml	18 fl oz	$2^1/_4$ cups
600 ml	20 fl oz	$2^1/_2$ cups
660 ml	22 fl oz	$2^3/_4$ cups
720 ml	24 fl oz	3 cups
780 ml	26 fl oz	$3^1/_4$ cups
840 ml	28 fl oz	$3^1/_2$ cups
900 ml	30 fl oz	$3^3/_4$ cups
960 ml	32 fl oz	4 cups

Ingredients in 1 cup

Ingredients	Metric	Imperial
Almonds, sliced	90 g	3 oz
Almonds, whole	150 g	5 oz
Butter	225 g	8 oz
Chocolate chips, mini	180 g	6 oz
Chocolate chips, regular size	180 g	6 oz
Chocolate cookie crumbs	120 g	4 oz
Cocoa powder	112 g	$3^3/_4$ oz
Dates	180 g	6 oz
Flour, cake	120 g	4 oz
Flour, plain (all-purpose)	120 g	4 oz
Graham cracker crumbs	120 g	4 oz
Hazelnuts	142 g	$4^3/_4$ oz
Macadamia nuts	142 g	$4^3/_4$ oz
Oil, olive	225 g	8 oz
Oil, vegetable	225 g	8 oz
Peanut butter	225 g	8 oz
Peanuts	142 g	$4^3/_4$ oz
Pecans	120 g	4 oz
Pineapple, crushed	225 g	8 oz
Raisins	180 g	6 oz
Rolled oats	105 g	$3^1/_2$ oz
Sugar, dark brown	225 g	8 oz
Sugar, granulated	200 g	7 oz
Sugar, icing (confectioner's)	120 g	4 oz
Sugar, light brown	225 g	8 oz
Vegetable shortening	172 g	$5^3/_4$ oz
Walnuts	120 g	4 oz

US Volume Equivalents

1 pint	=	2 cups
1 quart	=	2 pints
4 cups	=	1 quart
1 gallon	=	4 quarts